# HOME FRONT

*A true story based on the WWII diaries of Velma Beckerdite*

# HOME FRONT

# HOME FRONT

*A true story based on the WWII diaries of Velma Beckerdite*

*to George & Lori*

*Melinda B Hipple*

## Melinda B Hipple

IMPERIUM PUBLISHING
CREATE YOUR STORY

Home Front

Copyright © 2020 by Melinda B Hipple

ISBN: 978-1-64318-065-6

1097 N. 400th Rd
Baldwin City, KS, 66006
www.imperiumpublishing.com

This book is dedicated to my mother
and to all the women who served
their country in WWII by joining the
workforce. And for their greatest
sacrifice—losing those closest to them.

*I think when I start having my writings published, I'll send them to the best houses and say that I have read many books they've published and liked them—therefore I feel they could do my stories justice. Think I shall also send my baby picture. I had the look of someday being a writer. From the age of six months, I've been groping to know what the world's all about. But I'm human like all writers. None of them ever do."*

— VELMA BECKERDITE, 1947

# ONE

Vee clings tight to Jeanie's hand as they press their way through the crowd at Kansas City's Union Station.** It will be the last time she will see her best friend in many months, and she does not want to lose track of her before boarding the train.

On the platform, amid the acrid smell of diesel and hot metal, she turns to hug her friend. "Am I making a mess of this?"

"What do I know?" Jeanie asks. "But it certainly is an adventure!"

"I'm gonna miss you so much. Write lots." Vee loses her smile and adds, "I'll hope the best for Wayne when he marches through Hitler's front door."

"My brother will be fine," Jeanie assures her. "Both our brothers."

A strident voice rises over the din of goodbyes. "All aboard!"

As the friends push back from each other as far as the crowd will allow, Vee reaches up to touch the pale blue fascinator that holds back a strand of her thick black hair. "Thank you for this. It's beautiful. Now all the young men will take notice."

"You're getting married," Jeanie reminds her. "It's your new husband who should take notice."

A voice in the crowd calls, "Velma! Jeanie!" Two women squeeze past a man in uniform hugging a young child as a petite woman dabs a handkerchief to the corner of her eye. When Cora Long catches up to them, she thrusts her hand between two bystanders and offers Vee a small brown suitcase.

"You can't get to Idaho without your trousseau, now can you?"

"Oh, thank you, Mrs. Long! You are so good to bring me to the station." Vee gives her a one-armed hug and then squeezes the hand of Doris who has just arrived. She turns back to Jeanie. "I will write every day!"

With several backward glances, she makes her way to the nearest passenger coach and climbs the steps. She hugs the small suitcase to her chest and walks the narrow aisle. When she turns to make another pass, a solider stands and offers his seat.

"Oh, surely there's another one," she says, even though she knows there is not. He insists, so she tucks her luggage into the rack above their heads and settles near the aisle on the upholstered bench.

"I'm Jack," he says, offering his hand.

"Vee. Thanks."

The train lurches forward throwing the young man off balance, but he catches himself before falling into her lap. Vee turns to the window and scans the crowd for a familiar smile, but the mass of faces staring back at her are searching for someone else. She waves anyway. Just in case.

When the train crosses the state line and passes out of the city lights into the dark Kansas countryside, she turns her attention away from the window. Across the aisle, another young soldier sits with his wife and new baby. Vee remembers the family on the platform who, for whatever reason, had to part ways. At least this family has a few more hours or days, or perhaps weeks before the young husband and father marches off to an uncertain future. Vee stretches her hand out to wave at the child.

"She's very cute," she says when the mother nods appreciation. They make small talk for the next hour.

As the train pulls in to the Lawrence station, a handful of people leave the car. Vee slides toward the window, and Jack reclaims the open place on the bench. Somewhere in the middle of Kansas, Vee makes herself as comfortable as possible and drifts off to sleep.

At four in the morning, Jack nudges her awake. "Sorry. The conductor needs your ticket."

After it has been checked and punched, Vee returns the stub to her purse and closes her eyes again. The rumble of grinding iron and the swaying rhythm of the coach that, earlier, had lulled her to sleep now magnify her discomfort. Her legs begin to ache for room to stretch.

"Conductors are a lot of trouble," she mumbles when she notices Jack is still awake.

He nods. "I always wondered why they waited so long to check for tickets. We're almost to Denver."

"Is that where you're going?"

"Naw." He shifts toward her. "I'm headed to Victorville, California. Advanced Flying School." His shoulders square a bit. "I wanna be a pilot."

Vee starts to mention her bother, Eugene, but decides against it. Gene, too, had ambition to sit in the pilot's seat, but he did not make the cut. Still, he flies as a navigator.

"Where you headed?" Jack asks.

"Caldwell, Idaho. My fiancé is with the 311th there." Vee's cheeks flush heavily. She is surprised at how odd the word *fiancé* feels rolling off her tongue. It has been months since she made the decision to marry, but something leaves her unsettled when she thinks about her circumstance. Something she is not ready to admit to herself.

Turning away from Jack, she reaches into her purse and pulls out a small bundle of opened letters. Removing one from Jeanie's brother, she begins to reread.

*Dec 6, 1943*
*Camp Pickett*
*Dear Velma,*

*I haven't heard from you since I wrote last but I had to write to you again. I've been expecting a letter every day. If there was something in the last letter I wrote to you, I am awfully sorry. But I still see how wrong I was when I was at home before the army got me. Velma, it seems queer that a guy finds out too late things that he didn't know he wanted, isn't it. I bet you think I am silly and selfish, but honest Velma, I didn't realize lots of things that I know now. I wish I could see you once more before we go over. There are a few things I feel sure I could explain better.*

*I would love to hear from you. One thing more I would like to tell you before I close and go to bed. I want to thank you for how wonderful you were to me while I was home. I know there isn't any other girl around there I could have had half as much fun as I did with you.*

*Please write soon and let me know if I have hurt you, and please forgive me if I did. Love to a true friend,*
*Wayne*

The air in the train car grows heavy as Vee weighs her choices and the commitment she is making to just one man. She thinks back to her response to Wayne and to the concern that she could have lost a long-time family friend. But they had repaired the rift, though communication is still strained.

*Jan 4, 1944*
*Camp Pickett*
*Dear Velma,*

*I received your letter today, and I was a little surprised when you said you were going where Bob is and getting married. But it is the way, you say. There isn't any use in you kids being apart when you could be much happier together.*

*Say, you should be more careful about eating in the middle of the night. You might get indigestion.*

*No, I didn't cut those trees in the background of the picture. But one never can tell. I may be cutting trees if the captain catches me again. After all the time it took me to slip away from the corporals, just as I came in my barracks, the captain came in and he really blew up.*

*I was on guard Sunday night, and I liked to blew up myself, or rather it made me awfully unhappy. Cloudy as heck and raining like the very dickens. I walked for four hours in the rain. I got off guard at one o'clock in the morning. I came in to the mess hall and fried myself two big pork chops and an egg and drank two cups of coffee. I guess I had better practice what I preach about eating in the middle of the night, don't you think.*

*Well, I may as well close and write to the folks. But first I would like to wish you and Bob lots of happiness and good luck through your married life.*

*Love,*

*Wayne*

Vee slides both letters into their envelopes and tucks the bundle away. She thinks back to the week before, a little disgruntled that no one in the Long family had showed up at her surprise wedding shower—not even her best friend, Jeanie. She leans against the window and manages an uneasy sleep just before the train pulls into Denver.

At the station, Vee studies the familiar scene outside the window. Passengers board and disembark. Families, friends, lovers—some in uniform, some not—repeat the same tearful goodbyes she witnessed in Kansas City. Inside the coach, people play musical chairs with whatever seating they can find.

"War is good for business," Jack mumbles when the train pitches forward.

Vee nods. "Too bad it separates so many families."

At the mention of family, Jack pulls his wallet from a pocket and opens to a photo of him and a lovely young woman standing behind a young girl in a wheelchair. "My wife, Sarah, and our daughter, Martha. She came down with polio when she was just six months old."

"Oh, I'm very sorry to hear that." Vee's eyes dart from the photo to the baby across the aisle, and she watches the healthy, precocious child teethe on her daddy's dog tags. Looking back at Jack, she asks, "Will she get better?"

He shrugs and stuffs his wallet back into his pocket. "She gets physical therapy, but it's hard for her." His smile broadens. "She's sharp as a tack, though."

The train follows the eastern edge of the Rockies before turning west and ascending the first great pass. The views rival anything Vee has seen in picture books or on penny postcards. After sunset, she joins Jack and a couple of other soldiers in a few rounds of cards. When she can no longer keep her eyes open, she lays down on the bench and falls asleep.

Late the next morning, she wakes covered in an army overcoat.

"Mornin'," Jack says when she sits up. "You were talkin' in your sleep. Something about being cold. Oh, and I hope you don't mind. I gave the conductor your ticket last night so's not to wake you."

Vee pulls open her purse and makes a cursory glance at the contents. Everything is in order. "Thank you."

He tips his hat. "I'm off at the next stop. Been nice talking with you."

"You, too." She hands him his jacket.

In the hours before she reaches Caldwell, Vee tries her hand at cards again. The small group around her bores of the game, so a sergeant among them decides to entertain his fellow passengers with imaginary letters.

"Dear Department of War, If you think they are fighting in Europe, you should visit a Texas army camp!" All of the uniformed men in the coach burst into cheers and laughter.

At 2:45 the next morning, the train pulls into the Caldwell station. Vee retrieves her suitcase and steps onto the platform. After regaining her wobbly legs, she asks for directions to the Saratoga Hotel.

"Certainly," the clerk says. "It's a short walk."

She notes the directions and makes her way in the cold, dry air. In her room, she pulls off her coat and sits on the end of the bed. Directly across from her is a small desk backed by a tall ornate mirror. She studies her reflection—dark eyes, red lips, a milky complexion. After two days and nights on the train, her updo is falling out of its bobby pins, but no matter.

"I'm not the least bit tired." Noting a small stack of onionskin stationary and envelopes on the desk, she decides to write a few letters home.

*Dear Jeanie,*

> *Arrived safely in Caldwell. It's a simple town, but the people are friendly. I'm staying at a ritzy joint called the Saratoga. I have my own phone in my room! Sitting here at the desk, I still feel like I'm riding the train, like the room is rocking back and forth.*
>
> *I tried phoning Bob at the college tonight, but the operator refused to put the call through this late in the evening. Just imagine. Soon, I will be Mrs. Robert Beckerdite.*

She finishes the letter and pens a few more to friends and family. When her eyesight begins to blur, she changes into pajamas and crawls into bed.

***

The following afternoon, Vee explores the town center to locate the post office and a dime store where she buys a deck of cards. At the hotel, she tries once again to reach Bob, but has to leave a message. She brakes open the fresh deck and plays a few rounds of solitaire. When that fails to entertain, she grabs the copy of Gideon's Bible from the nightstand and starts reading. Deep in thought when the phone rings, her hand jerks and slings the book across the room.

"Velma? Hi. How are you?" Without waiting for an answer, Bob continues. "Sergeant Corn said you could stay with his family until you can find a room to rent. They're real nice folks. Even will let us have the wedding in their living room."

"Gee." Vee tries to sound enthusiastic. "That's really swell."

"They have an organ, and one of the lieutenants offered to play for us. It will be like a real wedding."

His last words sting. War requires great sacrifice from the men who serve, but the women and families not in uniform are making sacrifices of their own—some great, some small. Even a simple church wedding seems extravagant under the circumstances, but that does not ease Vee's ache for the fairy-tale moment.

"Do you get a pass tomorrow?"

"Sure do. I get the whole day. I'll call for you at the hotel in the morning before checkout."

After she hangs up, Vee sees her reflection in the mirror and makes a face. "I'm almost excited," she mumbles, "and for me, that's something."

The next morning, she stands waiting for Bob in the lobby. He arrives late, but meets her with a big kiss. "Maybe we should check back in," he suggests.

She dodges another kiss and scolds him. "Not until after the wedding." She hands him her suitcase. "We should go to the movies to keep out of trouble."

Bob holds the door for her. "We need to get our blood tests first."

They spend the afternoon at a double feature before driving to the Corns' home on the outskirts of Caldwell. Mrs. Corn welcomes them with generous hugs giving Vee a connection to something she has been missing. The Corns' daughter, Betty, is only a couple of years younger than Vee. And as much of a bookworm.

After a grand home-cooked meal, Betty shows them downtown Caldwell. It is twice the size of Vee's hometown, but the storefronts lack the historical character of a more established community. A few milkshakes and laughs later, and they return to the Corn home for a quiet evening beside the radio. When it is time for Bob to return to the dorm, Vee escorts him to the porch. He leans in for a goodbye kiss, pressing her hands together in the small of her back.

"See you tomorrow," he says, giving her one final kiss.

Vee steps back into the house and surveys the modest but comfortable home. Her own parents' house is a simple log home with few decorations—a reflection of her family's more modest lifestyle. By contrast, the Corns have furnished their home with an overstuffed sofa and chairs, and lovely custom draperies at each window. Vee is particularly impressed with Mrs. Corn's choice of artwork—something her parents seldom consider.

"He's handsome," Betty says when Vee sits next to her on the sofa. "And now he'll be a college man! You're very lucky."

"Maybe," she admits. "But the army has changed him."

"How so?"

"I don't know, exactly." She tries to shake her anxiety. "More sure of himself, perhaps."

Betty grabs Vee's hands and holds them tightly. "That's a good thing, isn't it? Now, tell me what you like to read."

# HOME FRONT

# TWO

**W**hen school is out, Betty and Vee attend a double feature nearly every afternoon. Vee shares her ideas for the wedding, and Betty introduces her to a host of new people from all walks of life. One couple is an Army cadet and his wife Ruth.

"I like Ruth a lot," Vee tells Betty later that evening.

"You sound surprised."

"I am, a little. I mean, she's Japanese."

Betty flops on the bed and pulls a pillow up to her chest. "They're just people. Ruth didn't start the war."

The clock in the living room chimes ten, reminding the girls it is time for bed. Vee moves to the door and closes it softly.

"What if she's a spy?" she asks with a wink. "She could tell someone about that cute college boy your parents are putting up."

"Maybe he's a spy, too!"

They both laugh at the thought, but Vee quickly sobers.

"My brother Eugene was a real college student before Pearl Harbor.

He wants to be a teacher. He quit to enlist." She walks to the dresser and pulls a packet from inside her suitcase. "Mom gave me some of the latest letters he wrote just before I left." She sits on the bed and pulls one from its envelope. With prompting from Betty, she begins to read.

> *Mac Dill Field*
> *January 12, 1944*
> *Dear Folks,*
>
> *This is my second letter to you today. I burned the other one—it was too bitter I noticed as I reread it. It is better not to get a load off your chest all at once, so I'll scowl awhile and write sensibly.*
>
> *I am sending you an income tax return. Send it on to where it should go.*
>
> *I am censoring my own letter, and I find plenty to censor, even on this second try.*
>
> *Would you send my shoes—the ones with strings only. Save the buckle shoes until I need them. Thanks.*
>
> *Love,*
>
> *Gene*
>
> *P.S. Dad, I gave you my power of attorney in case I'm missing in action.*

When she folds the letter back into place, she turns to Betty. "I know Mom thought the letters would be good for me so far from home, but this one worries me."

"Worries you how?"

"He seems so upset. And why did he have to talk about a power of attorney?"

Betty shrugs. "It's just a precaution, I'm sure. I bet all of the soldiers have to do it."

"Maybe." Vee tries to shake off the gloom. "I just hope Dad never has to use it."

***

Vee sleeps in the next morning. At lunch, a woman named Mrs.

LaBrier comes to visit and, afterward, drives Vee and Mrs. Corn to the post office to collect a parcel.

"Swell!" Vee exclaims on opening the box. "I will feel so much more at home with something else to wear."

They pick up a newspaper and search for a room Vee can rent while Bob is in training, but there appears to be nothing available. Though she and Betty Corn have become fast friends, she cannot share the room with Betty and her new husband when Bob has leave.

"There are so many young women just like yourself who are here for the men in training. Tell you what," Mrs. LaBrier finally says. "I have a room. I can do my part and let it to you for the time you are in Idaho."

"Oh, Mrs. LaB! That would be wonderful!" After they have agreed upon the rent, Vee leans in to give her a hug. "And since I'll be taking the third shift at the dehydrator plant, you won't hear a peep out of me most nights."

When school is out, Vee meets Betty at Cheeseboroughs for pie-a-la-mode.

"Mom said you asked for a shivaree," Betty says. "You know, in Europe, they used to use the shivaree to break up bad marriages."

Vee scrapes up the last bit of ice cream with her spoon and hopes her marriage will not be one of the bad ones. "Really? How do you know?"

"I read it. There were all sorts of awful things that people would do to each other."

"Well, I know it's not proper for me to be planning my own, but I love that your family is willing to do this for me." She pushes her plate away. "I'm just sorry my own family can't be a part of it."

Betty—fair complected with dark hair—could pass as Vee's sister. She tilts her head and stares at her roommate. "I think you're brave—coming so far from home to get married." She pushes her plate to the side and leans on the table. "Mom has a friend, Mrs. Chambers, who went all the way to China with her husband. They were missionaries."

"That is very brave!"

"I believe women can be just as brave as men."

Vee thinks about her brother flying as a navigator, and she shudders. "I don't know if I could do what Eugene is doing. Every time he goes up in the air, there will be Jerries and Japs who want to kill him. How can people be so horrid?"

A waitress comes to clear the table, so the girls pay for their pie and head home.

"I've been reading about politics," Betty says on the walk to the house. "There was this book, written by a Christian Democrat, and it just made me want to be a Republican."

"But the Democratic party is changing. Roosevelt has done so much for the people. He's the tops in my book."

They let the subject slide, but when they reach home, Sergeant Corn is in a good-hearted argument with a friend over politics even though they are arguing for the same thing.

When Mrs. Corn sees the girls, she rises from her chair. "Velma! Come in. There is someone you should meet." She escorts Vee into the living room. "This is Dr. Garrison, a minister." She dips her head and adds, "A Baptist."

She grasps Vee's elbow and pulls her closer. "Velma's staying with us because she's also a Baptist."

Betty leans into Vee's ear and whispers, "Only because you're a Baptist, I suppose."

"Well, it certainly isn't because I am a Democrat," Vee whispers back.

They enjoy another sumptuous meal before retreating to Betty's room.

"We should put up our hair tonight," Betty insists, and heads for the shower.

When Vee is alone, she digs into the box of clothing. From the very bottom, she pulls a large packet of opened letters along with a note.

> *More letters from Gene. I thought you would like to keep these with you.*
> *Love, Mom.*

"Oh, thank you!" she exclaims aloud. Hurrying to the bed, she pulls the rubber band off of the first stack and opens the top envelope. It is dated two years earlier. Vee has read it before, but it is the greatest gift she can imagine under the circumstances. She takes her time reading through the first bundle.

*Jefferson Barracks*
*May 27, 1942*
*Dear Folks,*

*Thanks for the money. I was down to 13 cents. Dad, there's no need to worry about my going into overseas service from this camp. Only general duty men (men not suited as specialists) could go from here. During classification, I qualified for practically every type of Army Air Corps technical school. I chose radio school.*

*The fellows here joke about the location of Army camps using this one as an example. They say an Army camp is always located where mice and rats won't even live.*

*We'll have a three or four-hour parade, today. Standing at attention or parade rest in the improper position cuts off blood circulation in the legs. Soldiers have been known to fall flat on their face at the command "Forward, march" after standing at attention for hours. Several persons drop out in every parade.*

*Write soon.*

*Gene*

*Patterson Field*
*July 15, 1942*
*Dear Folks,*

*Don't mind if dit-dahs show up in this letter. I'm dit-dah crazy from studying code.*

*Thanks for the after-shaving lotion and the cards. I had almost forgotten I had a birthday. I'm too busy to even think about anything but air-traffic rules and radio codes. I'll receive apprentice training in either control tower or airways radio, then Far East I go. In the meantime, I hope my flying cadet number comes up.*

*A plane's undercarriage was bent in a takeoff into a crosswind this morning. I don't believe the pilot was hurt.*

*I was paid this month. I think I'll have some of my pay deducted for defense bonds. Then, in case of foreign service, I would still be buying bonds.*

*Meanwhile, I really enjoy letters, though I don't have time to get homesick.*

*Gene*

*August 2, 1942*

*Dear Folks,*

*I'm on shipping orders to a flying field in Wisconsin as a student control tower operator, I think. It seems like I move every time I get used to a place. I'm continually adjusting myself to new conditions.*

*Gene*

*Camp Williams*

*August 7, 1942*

*Dear Folks,*

*Here I am in Wisconsin. Five of us came from Patterson Field to run the control tower here. This is a new army camp, very poorly equipped.*

*You'd like the country. The land is level and sandy, except for cliffs that rise almost vertically upward. The towns are small. The dells of the Wisconsin River are very unusual. I am sending some cards along to show you some of the scenic views.*

*I've had $25 per month of my pay taken out for defense bonds. I get a $100 bond every 3 months, because $75 buys it. I named Dad as beneficiary.*

*The food here isn't good. Yesterday our mashed potatoes had some sand in them. Some of the fellows were growling noticeably about it. I said, "Look at it this way. We need more bulk in our diet."*

*I'll send some money your way soon. From now on until I become a sergeant (one or two months, I hope) I won't have much spare cash. I expect to be a corporal within two weeks.*

*Did you ever hear about the W.A.A.C.S. who had just joined the army? They asked where they were supposed to eat. The army officer in charge replied, "You'll mess with the officers." The spokeswoman for the group replied, "Yes, I know, but where do we eat?"*

*Velma won't understand the jokes I send – they are so far above her mentality. Velma, are you sure you didn't bribe the health contest judges? H'm.*

*Velma, thanks for all that "trash." Thanks for the news. I must stop, stop, stop.*
*(I'm tower crazy now.)*
*Gene*

Vee laughs as she folds the letter away. Her older brother had been half a country away and still teasing her relentlessly.

Betty comes in dressed in her pajamas and her hair wrapped in a towel. "Your turn," she says when she lands on the bed.

With the letters tucked away, Vee heads for the bathroom to shower and wash her hair. Afterward, she and Betty take turns pin-curling each other's strands of long dark tresses. When they are done, Vee retrieves the letters and sits with Betty on the bed.

"Look what Mom sent! All of Eugene's letters from the last two years." She fans a few out for Betty to admire.

"Wonderful! A little piece of home."

"Yes, but they make me sad, too. I worry about him."

"Will you read some?" Betty asks as she touches one of the envelopes. "I'd like to know what it's like, being in the Army."

Vee pulls open another letter.

*Camp Williams*
*August 28, 1942*
*Dear Folks,*

*Here come 30 bucks. Do with it as you see fit.*

*I am a sergeant now—several months before I thought I would be. I jumped corporal rating. My salary jumped from $54 a month to $78. These three stripes look pretty good.*

*My service record is perfectly clean so far. A service record can be marred by circumstances beyond one's control. So I "walk straighter" than ever.*

*I have been notified that I have been placed on the priority register of enlisted men qualified for aviation cadet training. So maybe I'll be flying after all before this year is over.*
*Gene*

"Oh, he sounds so wonderful," Betty says when Vee moves to the next letter. "Dreamy, in fact." She crawls under the covers and waits for Vee to start again.

*Nashville, Tennessee*
*September 17, 1942*
*Dear Folks,*

*Don't answer this. Your letter would only be delayed.*

*You will be receiving a money order from a fellow named Chirgwin for $15. He borrowed it from me before I was sent here. He is going to send it to you. Keep it – Dad, get some teeth pulled. Dad, that's an order, see?*

*This is a classification center for pilots, navigators, and bombardiers. I hope I'll be a pilot, but with my mathematics I'll probably come out navigator—king of the ship. I may not be home until I get wings and bars – become a flying officer.*

*I'm sending you some pictures. You may enjoy them. I know I will after this mess is over. The larger picture is some of the fellows at Patterson Field. There are men from almost every walk of life. Rogers was an office worker in St. Louis who sung in a St. Louis opera company. Beautiful tenor voice. Rubenstein was a lawyer with 6 years of college. A talking terror. Chirgwin worked in a factory in Flint, Michigan. Samson, not yet an American Citizen, in the Army through special conditions with selective service system. Wants to fly when he becomes a citizen. Knows and speaks German, French, and English. Came to America from Germany six years ago. Hates Hitler and what Hitler does. Has been over half the world and is highly brilliant and well-educated. Before Hitler, his family was one of the best known in Germany. Wing Chinn, a Chinese boy, American citizen. Wants to fly. Can read and write Chinese and English.*

*Last, but not least, I should say something of Sylvia. She was one of several "swell" girls I became acquainted with in Wisconsin. As you can see from the picture, she is . . . well, she has everything.*

*I am very unsettled here as yet. It may be a week or two before I get an address that could be called an address.*

*Gene*

*September 24, 1942*

*Dear Folks,*

 *I have passed my physical for flying. Is it tough? Whew! I had to take a complete neurological examination, too, because I mentioned that I had headaches two weeks after I had the measles three years ago. Measles, it seems, sometimes affects the nervous system. A person has to be close to absolutely normal in every respect to pass the army's flying examination. I don't believe I would have passed coming out of civilian life. But the Army has done me good. Changes in surroundings don't shock me. I have decided to ask for navigator rather than pilot because navigation will be a much better field after the war. My eyes are too good. I'll probably come out pilot. The next few days will tell the story. The navigator gets to fly, anyway. The Army will put me where I fit best, I hope. Navigators usually go to California from here.*

 *Velma, you're as crazy as ever. For example, you call a beautiful girl like Sylvia merely "cute." H'm.*

 *Is this letter ever disorganized? Yas, yas.*

 *Gene*


"He's funny, too," Betty says. "But he has a girlfriend!" She feigns a look of dismay.

"Oh, he's had several," Vee says, laughing. "He's a regular playboy!" She opens the next envelope.


*October 3, 1942*

*Dear Folks,*

 *Thanks for the letters and news. Velma, that's fairly good. "She was shaped like an hourglass, and she made every minute count." Is it original? Honestly, I doubt it. Ho! Ho! Ha! Ha! I laughed.*

 *If I am classified as navigator, I can get my wings in about five months. I may not get home until then.*

 *Gene*

Vee puts away the letter. "He kept promising he'd get home, but the Army just moved him to another base. We didn't see him until last fall."

"I'm sorry," Betty says, making a face.

"One more letter. You have school tomorrow!" Vee pulls the pages from their hiding place and begins once more.

*October 6, 1942*

*Dear Folks,*

*I've just been classified as pilot. Pilots are badly needed. I am almost certain I was better qualified as navigator. However, I had agreed to let them put me where they wanted me. So pilot I shall try to become. My training will be at least seven months for wings and bars. I don't care where I fly—pilot, navigator, or bombardier—as long as I can knock down some Japs.*

*Thanks for that nice fat letter. It was full of news and, in Velma's case, a lot of goofy material. Velma, that goofy stuff tain't bad – tain't good. Fact is, it's tainted.*

*I talk too fast for some of these Southerners. Harry Rubenstein, that fellow who worked with me at Camp Williams and who is now taking officer candidate training for administration in the Air Corps and who was a lawyer in Chicago in civilian life, would talk ten times too fast for anybody. We called him "Horrible Harry, the Chicago Cyclone."*

*Well, I better stop. I'm rambling too much.*

*Gene*

"Bedtime," Vee says, and she places the packet of letters on top of her suitcase. "I should be thinking about my wedding."

"And your husband-to-be."

"Yes. And Bob." She turns out the light and crawls in beside her roommate.

# THREE

**I**n the morning, Vee spends time reading bits of the many books the Corns keep in their library. After lunch, she takes the blood test results to the courthouse and picks up the marriage license. The wedding is two days away.

The thought of being married both excites and unnerves her. Bob is from a good family. He is hard-working and should be a good provider, but if Vee is honest with herself, she cannot say she is truly in love. At least not the storybook romance she has hoped for. But her fiancé can be loads of fun. Surely, they will manage to build a good life together.

At the post office, she finds another letter from her mother with an additional one from Eugene. She makes her way to a quiet table in a nearby café and opens them. After digesting the news from home, she pulls out her brother's newest letter.

*Mac Dill Field*
*January 23, 1944*
*Dear Folks,*

*Just as soon as Velma gets located, would you send me her address. If I were in her shoes, I would do as she did.*

*We have shirt-sleeve weather—on the ground. At high altitude yesterday, I knocked icicles out of my oxygen mask.*

*No, I wasn't fined. I sometimes think I'm too much "on the beam" in some respects. When I wrote that last letter, I was in the worst mood I've been in since I've been in the army. I don't know how much longer we will be in the U.S., probably anywhere from one to three months. We are practically ready.*

*I was out with a Spanish girl last week. Ordinarily Spanish girls don't appeal to me, but this one – ah! I am all for seeing her again, but my bombardier says no. He says women are like socks, they should be changed twice a week. Fat chance I have of changing them twice a week when I only find time to leave the post three times a month.*

*Love,*
*Gene*

When Vee arrives home, Betty is already waiting. She shares the latest letter and the fact that Eugene has another girlfriend.

"Oh, poo," Betty complains from the bed. She kicks off her shoes and shrugs. "No matter. I don't think I'll ever get married."

"Why would you say that?"

"Well, I want to go away somewhere and be different altogether."

Vee laughs. "Different how?"

"Maybe I'll change my name and become a doctor. Not just a nurse. I mean, why not?"

"Maybe you could become a missionary like Mrs. Chambers. But without the *Mrs.*" Vee imagines that Betty can do anything she makes up her mind to. She is the first person Vee has ever wanted to envy, and yet Betty will not let her. She is too self-effacing.

"I like that idea!" Betty says, wrapping herself in her quilted spread.

"Read me some more of Gene's old letters, please. I feel like I'm getting to know him, too."

Vee pulls more envelopes from her suitcase and opens them.

*October 8, 1942*

*Dear Folks,*

*I don't recommend the following instructions on "What to do in case of an air raid," and if you carry them out, you do so at your own risk.*

*1. As soon as bombs start dropping, run like hell. (It doesn't matter where you run, as long as you run like hell.) If you are inside a building, run outside. If you are outside, run inside.*

*2. Take advantages of opportunities afforded you when air raid sirens sound the attack warning—for example:*

*a. If in a bakery, grab some pie, cake, etc.*

*b. If in a tavern, grab a bottle.*

*c. If in a movie, grab a blonde.*

*3. If you find an unexploded bomb, always pick it up and shake it like hell, the firing pin may be stuck.*

*4. If an incendiary bomb is found burning in a building, throw some gasoline on it. You can't put it out anyway, so you might just as well have some fun:*

*a. If no gasoline is available, throw a bucket of water on it and lie down, you're dead.*

*b. The properties of the bomb free the hydrogen from the water with rather rapid combustion. (In fact, it will explode with a helluva crash.)*

*5. Always get excited and yell bloody murder. It will add to the fun and the confusion and scare hell out of the kids.*

*6. Smoke your ripest pipe, drink heavily, eat onions, Limburger cheese, etc., before entering a crowded air raid shelter. This will make you unpopular with the crowd in your immediate vicinity, eliminating any unnecessary discomfort that would be more prevalent if people crowded too closely.*

*7. If you should be the victim of a direct bomb hit, don't go to pieces—lie still and you won't be noticed. Ha! Ha!*

*Gene*

Betty scowls from the covers. "I know he meant that to be funny, but it's scary, too."

"I try not to think of it," Vee says as she folds the letter away. Her brother has always had a great sense of humor, but she realizes how much more she appreciates it now that the war has put him in harm's way. "Maybe this one will be better."

*October 19, 1942*
*Dear Folks,*

*I am restricted to the post now. The next time I leave the post, I leave it for good. I am on shipping orders—to where I don't know. I hope to go to California.*

*I wonder if you can read this. This writing on a bunk is the bunk. Velma won't like that last statement—it's not good, but how much better can I do? I tried, anyway.*

*My next letter will come from elsewhere.*

*Gene*

*Maxwell Field, Ala.*
*October 24, 1942*
*Dear Folks,*

*I arrived here the 20th. I am in pre-flight class 43F. For four weeks I will be an under-classman, and is this life tough. They are trying to give us what West Pointers get in four years in only nine months. We are at attention almost all the time. We even eat at attention—chest against table, shoulders braced, head back, chin in, and left arm at side, also, eyes on a fixed point. I may live four weeks.*

*This was a swell mail day. I got two letters from home and one from Aunt Clara. That gob of junk Velma sent was a mess, gee whiz!*

*I had thought I might get home Christmas. I don't believe I will get home now. I'm still hoping, though.*

*I haven't gotten a wristwatch yet. I should before I get to flight school. A pilot can get the time from a wristwatch without taking a hand off the controls.*

*Here's an interesting fact. A flying officer costs the army about 30,000 dollars. In pre-flight school we actually receive officer training, and is it tough? They try to get your temper to blow up. The idea is to train us to take anything calmly. We get gigged when we don't follow all cadet regulations (we can't follow them all). Gigs give us demerits. We are given five free demerits each week. If we get more than five in a week we have to walk punishment tours (we'll all probably walk some tours).*

*Our appearance has to be perfect—cleanly shaven, fingernails absolutely clean, hair cut short, uniform clean, shirt tucked in a certain way, our brass shined, shoes shined, and socks held in place with garters (darn 'em).*

*The following will give you an idea how we have to answer upperclassmen:*

*Upperclassman: "Sound off, mister." Underclassman: "Sir, new aviation cadet Hammontree, E. L., sir."*

*Upperclassman: "Pop to, mister." Whereupon the underclassman comes to attention so fast there is a pop of shoe against shoe.*

*Upperclassman: "Make a nasty move, mister." Such a command comes when an underclassman is already at attention. The underclassman comes to an exaggerated position of attention.*

*There are only three standard answers in a cadet corps – Yes, sir; No, sir; and No excuse, sir.*

*Upperclassman: "Are you on the ball, mister?" Underclassman: "Sir, I am firmly established on that well-known spherical object, sir." "Wrack 'em back, misters" – in other words, pull back your shoulders until your shoulder blades touch in your back. "Hit the rat line, misters" – the rat line is a six-inch path along the stoops of our barracks. We have to walk on this line in 15-inch steps at a rate which is almost a run.*

*They keep us busy from 5 A.M. until 9:30 P.M. every day. Technically, we get Sunday off. Actually, we don't. The army has kept me busy ever since I walked into that recruiting room at Kansas City and signed my name on the dotted line. I've learned a lot, though. The main issue at stake now is to toughen up for flying so that I can help knock down some Japs.*

*Write.*

*Gene*

*November 7, 1942*

*Dear Folks,*

*I got your package before I got your letter – the army mail system. Thanks from me (and the other five "misters" in my room) for that box of oatmeal cookies. Yum, Yum!*

*The nervous tension is very high here. Some cadets snap under the strain. One of our cadets "snapped/told off" an upper classman and immediately asked to be put back to private, unassigned. The most important thing in our cadet training is to control our temper absolutely. We are trained to stand at attention and be insulted at the same time. I am lucky there. I have very little trouble controlling my temper.*

*Good for you, Dad, I'm glad you broke down and wrote. I'm sure going to fight for a chance to get home Christmas. This year I'll be too far from home to hitch it in just a few hours.*

*Oh, Velma, in Jeanie's last letter, this appeared. "P.S. Write soon and don't forget it. This is a last warning." Velma, could you decode that? Am I about to come to an untimely end? In other words, do I need a bodyguard? Seriously, tell Jeanie thanks and bid her continue in her good works. Tell her t'anks for the ink and splatter me with some more soon.*

*Gene*

The girls go in to help Mrs. Corn with dinner. After they finish eating, Vee clears the table. In the kitchen, Mrs. C takes her by the shoulders.

"A young friend of ours is having a wedding shower tomorrow night. Why don't you come?"

"Oh, that would be wonderful!" Vee says, excited to be included. "You've been so nice to me. Just like family."

Mrs. C puts the last of the dishes into the cupboards. "I dare say, Betty thinks of you as family now. She'll miss you when you move to Mrs. LaBrier's."

Vee hangs the dishtowel over its bar to let it air dry. "Don't worry. I will come see her whenever I can. Growing up with all brothers, it's nice to know what it's like to have a sister."

\*\*\*

Friday morning, Vee crawls out of bed just in time to finish a breakfast of cold French toast and syrup before she runs off to her hair appointment. Too anxious to head back to the house, she stops at the café to have coffee and pie before Betty shows up after school.

"Tomorrow's the big day," Betty says. "You can get some pointers at the shower tonight. We're having a mock wedding." She tosses her head high. "I'm the groom."

"Oh, lordy! That will be something to see."

"Yes, and Margaret Slack is the bride. She's carrying a bouquet of lovely radishes down the aisle."

After the shower, they crawl into bed and try several times to end their conversation before sleep.

"Doris received some swell wedding gifts tonight, didn't she?"

"Oh, yes. They were swell, alright."

"And your big day is tomorrow. Are you excited?"

Vee tries to sort out all the emotions she feels. "Of course! I don't know where to start."

When Betty turns to her in the dark and says, "Just remember to say 'I do' when it's your turn," they both laugh loud enough to get a stern warning from the living room.

"Night."

# HOME FRONT

# FOUR

O n the morning of the 29th, the temperature has climbed to just below freezing. But even with a light breeze, Vee is comfortable. Betty accuses her of being hot for her beau.

"It's going to be so much fun," Betty declares before her expression sobers. "But I'm going to miss you."

"I'm not going far. And if I'm working nights, I can sleep in the morning and then see you after school. It will be perfect!"

Bob comes from the base around 1:30 in the afternoon, and he and Sergeant Corn move the living room furniture into rows with an aisle leading to the fireplace. Mrs. Corn brings in two lovely vases of flowers and places them on either side of the mantle. After Vee gives her approval, she slips into the shared bedroom to prepare for the wedding.

"Here," Betty says, handing her an embroidered handkerchief. "Something borrowed. Do you have everything else?"

Vee turns around for inspection. "My *new* suit that Mom bought, an *old* Indian head penny in my shoe, and the *blue* fascinator that my friend Jeanie gave me."

"Perfect! You are a beautiful bride."

Vee sends her friend out to start the ceremony. A few minutes later, there is a light tap on the door.

"Velma? Are you ready?"

She opens the door to Sergeant Corn standing in his uniform. "I'm here to escort you," he says with some manner of pride. "I hope I'm not too poor an excuse for your own father."

"Oh, not at all." She takes his arm.

On cue, Mrs. Corn begins to play the *Wedding March* on the family's organ. When Vee enters the room, she sees her handsome groom beaming from ear to ear in his own dress uniform. Beside him stands the best man, Robert Artz. Betty Corn stands as bridesmaid.

Halfway through the ceremony, a Miss Betts sings a beautiful rendition of *Because*—as beautiful as any Vee has heard on the radio.

"I now pronounce you husband and wife!"

Everyone in the room stands and cheers as Bob tips his wife over his arm for a long kiss.

The small group moves into the dining room while the newlyweds prepare to cut the wedding cake. The guests take their slices and find seats around the house. In a private moment, Betty and Vee eye the best man.

"I think Mr. Artz is a bit tight," Vee says under her breath.

Betty giggles. "Maybe he has a flask hiding in his jacket." She hooks her arm through the bride's and adds, "Congratulations, by the way. Mrs. Beckerdite."

In the moments that follow, Vee watches the people in the room exchange stories and well wishes. She thinks of home and what her family has missed. As conversations turn political, her thoughts turn to her brother. Not only is Gene missing her wedding, but he has spent another Christmas away from family. Always, duty pulls him farther from home. Through his letters, she is developing a deeper appreciation for the man he has become—even if he did continue to tease her relentlessly.

Bob finds her staring wistfully at Sergeant and Mrs. Corn.

"I hope we are that happy someday," she tells him.

"You're not happy now?" he asks.

She leans into his shoulder and murmurs, "Oh, yes. This is the happiest day of my life."

***

The couple spends their honeymoon night at the Saratoga Hotel. In the morning, Bob's cousin Lee drives them to Uncle Willard and Aunt Anna Donaldson's farm for a home-cooked meal. Vee can barely see the two-story farmhouse shrouded in trees and shrubs. Across the dirt drive stands a number of freshly-painted barns and outbuildings. Between the barns and the road, an acre of discarded machinery and household items litter the field. Vee notices a rusting Model T Ford at one edge of the yard.

"Welcome to the home place," Lee says, opening the door to his newest Model T—still twenty years old. "Mom's got a real spread waiting for us." He escorts them into the dark interior of the home.

"Quaint," Vee says to Bob when they are seated at the kitchen table. "I noticed an electric stove out in the dump. It looks brand new."

Lee overhears. "Mom tried to learn to cook on it, but she kept burning everything. We finally put her wood stove back where she wanted it."

Vee cannot argue with Anna's cooking. It tastes like home.

Willard takes them on a tour of the farm. It is many times larger than her father's forty acres. She envies the wide stretches of farmland edged by distant mountain slopes. Her own father had once owned a larger parcel of land, but gave much of it to the bank during the depression. He had provided for the family, but Vee still recalls those hungry days. At least her father tills his fields with a tractor and not the draft horses Willard still uses.

After a quiet afternoon talking farming and the war effort, Lee drives them back to the Corns' to pack Vee's things and move her to Mrs. LaBrier's home on Blaine Street. Vee says her goodbyes to Betty and promises to meet her after school later in the week.

"And you'll bring Eugene's letters, won't you?"

"Certainly!"

Bob helps Vee settle into her room. He spends a final few moments stealing kisses from his new bride before returning to campus for the week ahead.

The new Mrs. Beckerdite finishes straightening the room that will be her home for the next several months. When it is time for bed, she pulls out her diary and fills the relevant page.

"Dear Diary, Today, I'm an old married woman, they tell me. Well! So what!?? I like it." She switches her writing to shorthand. "Did I sleep last night? No. Bob was either kidding me or expressing sweet nothings into my little ears. Well, ain't we got fun!!!" And back to cursive. "Am I thankful I took shorthand!"

She closes out the entry and tucks the book away. The evening quiet magnifies the emptiness of the room. Unable to fall asleep, she turns to the comfort of her brother's old letters.

*Maxwell Field, Ala.*
*November 21, 1942*
*Dear Folks,*

*We became upperclassmen yesterday. Those who will become our underclassmen would shiver if they knew what they are to receive at our hands. I got through underclass without walking any punishment tours (common, in a cadet's life). I hope such be true in upperclass.*

*No longer do we eat at attention. I may get to flight school yet. I may even be an army flyer yet, who knows.*

*Thanks for all those letters and all that news. Harold Dean, I'll bet you look queer in glasses. And yes, I do write to Sylvia—not necessarily as you suggested.*

*Did you ever hear about the man who moved to the city because he heard the country was at war?*

*WRITE*

*Gene (news-hungry)*

*November 26, 1942*

*Dear Folks,*

This is the end of Thanksgiving Day. We had a big dinner today at the mess hall—turkey, cold ham, potatoes, sweet potatoes, grapefruit cocktail, pie, cake, ice cream, nuts, etc.

Did I say this letter would be longer than the previous one? It won't. Time is chasing me. Here's hoping I have something to write next time.

*Anyway,*

*Gene*

*December 13, 1942*

*Dear Folks,*

At last I found time to write. We took our high altitude chamber test last Thursday. We went to a simulated (artificial) altitude of 18,000 feet, where the air pressure is one-half normal, without oxygen; then on to 28,000 feet, with oxygen, and where the air pressure is less than one-third normal. We had to keep swallowing to keep the air pressure on the ear-drum balanced to keep it from bursting. Those of us who do well on this test are better suited as bomber pilots because long-range bombers fly at high altitudes.

I still hear rumors of furloughs. If we go on to flying school without getting home, we will have been gypped.

*As usual,*

*Gene*

*December 16, 1942*

*Dear Folks,*

It seems that I'm not going to get home for Christmas. Our schedule is already planned up to December 27. We'll leave here before the new year starts.

I am sending you thirty dollars for Christmas. I don't know how much the army owes me. I have been paid on a regular payroll only once. I have been moved so much I suppose my service records are lost.

*MERRY CHRISTMAS*

*Gene*

The letters that should reassure Vee only serve to frustrate her more. She turns out the light and tries to fall asleep, but the many uncertainties in her life keep sending her into awkward dreams that jolt her awake. Sometimes she is flying just above the ground, struggling to keep herself in the air. Sometimes she is standing on the outside of a house, looking through a window to see the people she loves just out of reach. Many of the faces in her dreams are strangers to her—with Asian features or in uniform.

***

She spends the next morning writing letters to everyone she knows. After lunch, Mrs. LaB drives them into the country to fit a woman with a Spirella corset.

"You know, with your figure," her landlady tells her, "we should fit you for one, too. You'd look exquisite, my dear."

Vee turns up her nose at the idea of living inside a full-body corset, wired into place. Besides, her waist is already so small that her new husband can touch his thumbs and fingers when he places them around her middle.

On the way back to town, they stop at the post office where Vee drops seventeen letters into the outgoing mail. After picking up groceries, they head home where Betty is waiting.

"How about we wear our corsages one more time before they wilt. There's a great double feature on." The two girls dress in their finest once more and sit through *Girl Crazy* and *Dr. Gilespie's Criminal Case*. At Cheeseboroughs, they order Cokes and burgers.

"How does it feel to be married?"

Vee rolls her eyes. "I can't tell you everything!" After they stop giggling, she adds, "It's swell, I guess. It doesn't feel real, yet. Maybe when the war is over and we make a real home together."

"Do you like it at Mrs. LaBrier's house?"

"Oh, she's swell! But I miss my roommate." She winks at Betty. "It's so quiet there at night, just her and me in the house. Still, there's lots to read, just like at your place."

Betty finishes off her burger and lets the waitress take the plate. "Tomorrow, I'm coming over to hear more letters. Even if Gene does talk about this Sylvia person too much."

# HOME FRONT

# FIVE

**The week brings little mail from home.** Vee insists she is not homesick, but she misses the news of family and friends. When Jeanie does finally write, the news brakes her heart.

"My Uncle Raymond passed away," she tells Betty that evening at the cafe. "And no one in my family could write to tell me?"

"Maybe they are so busy with arrangements and the funeral."

"He was my favorite uncle." Vee pushes her plate away.

"I'm so sorry."

"He had been sick a long time. Ever since he came back from the first war. Maybe it's better he's gone." She picks at her fries. "Jeanie said they wouldn't give Dude leave to attend the funeral. I wonder where in the world he is tonight. And Gene. And Wayne."

When she remembers the reason her and Betty agreed to meet, her eyes light up. "I did bring more letters to share. I think the last one you heard was from Alabama. Then they moved him to Arkansas!"

*Helena Aero-Tech*
*December 29, 1942*
*Dear Folks,*

*I've moved again—closer to home for a change. Not close enough to ever be able to get home, however. I arrived here yesterday, traveling by rail from Maxwell Field. We were issued our flight clothing and equipment today. Tomorrow we start flying. War pressure is on. We'll learn to fly good in a hurry (the Army way) or wash out.*

*This is a civilian school contracted by the army. We have civilians as instructors, army officers in charge. Discipline is strict. I didn't think it would be in flying school. Our flight clothing is unusually warm. Fully dressed, only a small part of the pilot's face is exposed. Our overshoes are even thickly padded with wool. I look like a stuffed toad in my outfit.*

*Time is still precious. It seems that a flying cadet never has any free time. I hope such is not the case all the way through, if I go through.*

*Gene*

*January 1, 1943*
*Dear Folks,*

*Flying the Army way is very hard work. Dad, you know what I always said about rather being in an airplane than on the roof of a two-story building. I still say so. I've been up three times now with a total of 2 hours and 20 minutes army flying time. I like it up there. I have no fear of an airplane. We have to learn so fast I'm in a daze. Objects really look different viewed from an airplane than viewed from the ground. I could easily get lost up there in the blue. I hope I learn this stuff fast enough not to wash out. Many good flyers in civilian life even wash out.*

*The plane we are learning in would have been termed a "hot" plane during the last war. It lands at 80 miles per hour with landing flaps. It's a Fairchild PT-19A low-wing monoplane with characteristics of larger planes.*

*No one seems suspicious of us or unfriendly. You would be surprised how many cold stares a soldier can get from those who are doing nothing for their country.*

*Gene*

*January 6, 1943*

*Dear Folks,*

   *I have seen a lot of the army in a few months – buck private, non-commissioned officer, and now, flying cadet and, I hope later, flying officer.*

   *People are very friendly. We cadets almost have to fight every time we go to Helena to keep those of the feminine sex at a safe distance.*

   *I am trying to learn to fly so hard that I almost lose the airport. There are so many things to do at once—feet on rudders, one hand on stick, one hand on throttle, watch other planes, hold desired altitude, hold desired airspeed, keep engine revving at the desired speed, hold course, and at the same time not break any of the multitude of flying regulations the army imposes—and demands not be broken.*

   *Before we solo, we learn all that is necessary to fly a plane. Takeoff, landing, shallow turns, medium turns, and steep turns, climbing turns, gliding turns, six kinds of stalls, and spins and recovery therefrom. Each of these is done a special way—the army way. To learn to fly the army way is seemingly hopeless, but some of us will do it.*

   *Our food is excellent. The best I've ever had in the army. Civilians run the mess hall—that explains such whole-some, well-cooked food.*

   *Stopping abruptly,*

   *Gene*

*January 10, 1943*

*Dear Folks,*

   *Your package arrived. Thanks. I shall smoke one cigar as I study German aircraft tonight.*

   *I am not washed out yet. I plan to solo within the next two days. The hardest part of flying (for me) is setting the plane down easily. It's easy to get these planes off the ground—they almost naturally take to the air.*

   *Slow rolls are fun—when you're hanging upside down in the safety belt. To show how complicated flying is, when a plane's wings are vertical, the actions of most of the controls are either interchanged or reversed. So far, I haven't been sick upstairs yet.*

   *I have been appointed a member of the honor board. All officers and cadets of the army live by a rigid honor code. Those proved guilty of breaking the honor code cannot be officers. It's an honor to be on the board—yet judging honor is a tough proposition. I don't relish it.*

*I went to the Baptist church in West Helena this morning.*
*Still hating two-story roofs as,*
*Gene*

Betty interrupts. "He must really be something to be on the honor board."

Vee nods. "I've never thought of him as anything but my older brother until now."

Eugene had always looked out for his little sister when they were young, but he could drive her crazy with his constant insults. She realizes, now, that his teasing is an expression of affection. The longer they are separated by distance, the more his letters bring them together.

*Helena, Arkansas*
*January 21, 1943*
*Dear Folks,*

*There is not any thrill in army flying. The thrill is replaced by demanded precision from the first ride. One false move and you're out. So far as for being up in the air and flying the plane, I like it.*

*Here's a good true story from Nashville. A cadet was being classified. He was asked if he had ever been up in a plane. He answered that he had been up six times. He was asked how he liked landing. He answered that he had never landed in a plane. He was called back for a re-check – they thought he was "off." He gave the same answer as before, then explained that he had been a para-trooper and had been required to make six jumps.*

*All kinds of funny things have happened to us. One fellow went up without fastening his safety belt. He was lucky because he was not inverted. He might have pulled silk ("jumped" to you). He was sweating blood part of the time and grabbing everything in the cockpit that was solid and some things that weren't. We had plenty of fun at his expense.*

*Pull silk – jump parachutically (my own word).*

*We have excellent food, good medical care, and very comfortable double-decker beds. I wish we had more time to use our beds.*

*Write to,*
*Gene*

*January 24, 1943*

*Dear Folks,*

　*As a cadet, I get $10,000 in free life insurance, so I put the $2,000 one out of force.*

　*At last I know what cooks. I'm washed out as pilot. I have found that I was also classified as navigator at Nashville. Therefore, I still fly. This flying game is the most uncertain thing in the army.*

　*Velma, if most of that stuff you last wrote is original, you're a comedian.*

　*T'ANKS*

　*Gene*

*January 28, 1943*

*Dear Folks,*

　*We had a snow (or rather, sleet) here three days ago. It stopped flying for two days.*

　*I'm including $11 in this letter. I guess this will be the last money I'll send for a while. Someone relieved me of twenty bucks I had in a drawer. It should have been safe. Cadets never steal. If I can, I want to send a money order for twenty dollars and you to reserve it for me in case I need it.*

　*I want to be a navigator on a B17E – the Flying Fortress – the same plane I wanted to pilot.*

　*Landing as,*

　*Gene*

Vee returns the letters to her purse. "That's the last one he sent from Arkansas. Then they moved him again."

When the young women finish their drinks, they walk to the Corn home where Bob has left an address. Vee thanks them for taking the message and then heads back to Mrs. LaB's. After setting her hair and listening to the Fred Waring radio show, she reads herself to sleep.

# HOME FRONT

# SIX

**The Thursday morning rain sets in for the day.** Vee rouses occasionally to hear the rhythm of water dripping from the eaves. After reading a letter from Bob, she follows directions to the address she had been given the day before.

"Welcome!" Mrs. Basie opens the door wide to welcome her guest. "Did you get a ride?"

"No." Vee closes her umbrella before stepping inside. "I love walking in the rain."

"Well, you should come in and get warm. Ruth is in the living room." Mrs. Basie takes Vee's coat and ushers her through a lovely arched doorway.

In the living room, Ruth Fox sits demurely on the edge of a floral sofa and holds a delicate teacup and saucer in her lap. "Coffee?" she asks when Vee sits across from her.

They exchange pleasantries before relaxing into a deeper conversation. Before long, Vee has lost track of time. More surprising to her is the fact that she no longer sees Ruth as Japanese despite her obvious Asian features.

The more they talk, the more they find their interests and ideologies overlap.

"Bob wrote me today that his sister, Norma, has scarlet fever."

Ruth and Mrs. Basie both proclaim their sincere hopes for a speedy recovery, while Mrs. Basie adds, "You be careful getting chilled in the rain. We don't want you getting sick, as well."

Their hostess checks the hall clock and stands. "You must stay for lunch. We can talk about the dehydrator before I go on shift. The plant is always looking for help, but I'll warn you, it's not easy work."

"How so?"

Mrs. Basie shares a knowing look with Ruth. "Let's just say, if you get past the first couple of days, you'll do fine."

All through lunch, Vee tries to pry more information out of her, but Mrs. Basie refuses to say more than a few words about the plant. They finish their meal and spend the rest of the afternoon sharing stories of family and friends affected by the war.

Just before 4:00, Mrs. Basie leaves for work, and Vee bids Ruth goodbye, having gained a new perspective on the idea of race. They are just people, she keeps reminding herself as she makes her way home in a deluge of winter rain.

Mrs. LaB is off fitting someone new for a corset, so Vee has the house to herself. She wonders what Betty is up to, and then remembers her after-school practice on Thursdays. For the first time since she arrived in Idaho, Vee feels homesick.

"No letters from home today," she complains to the emptiness. "Perhaps they've forgotten me." All of the war talk earlier inspires her to dig out more of Gene's letters. She finds a quiet corner and opens a new bundle.

*Nashville Army Air Center*
*February 20, 1943*
*Dear Folks,*

*I arrived here the 10th at night by rail from Helena. It seems that I'm going to be a navigator after all.*

*I got the package all right. We (all 30 of us in the barracks) enjoyed the cookies.*

*I am sending a package of stuff home. Maybe Harold Dean can have some fun with my watch—it's been slung around some in a barracks bag over almost half the United States. I bought a fair wrist watch before I went to primary. It's a shock-proof Swiss watch. Cost $23. I wear it everywhere except in the shower.*

*We pilot washouts have it swell here. We have no K.P. or guard duty as other squadrons. We are not quarantined. We have academics and P.T. (physical training).*

*I'll be leaving in less than a week, I think. I don't know whether I'm leaving as navigator or bombardier. I'm classified as a navigator, but today I filled out confidential forms that a bombardier has to fill out. The bombardier works with the secret Norden bomb sight. His character has to be that desired.*

*Oh, yes, Mom, when I said you could sling ink, I meant you could do a good job of sending news. Nothing ever happens to me now that I can call exciting news. The army has made me adapt myself to so many different things one after the other.*

*Landing as,*
*Gene*

*February 26, 1943*
*Dear Folks,*

*Your letter did pretty good—Parsons, Kansas to Helena, Arkansas to Nashville, Tennessee and to me in just three days. That speed is unusual. George Washington's birthday was just another day to the army.*

*Oh, yes, my blind date. She wasn't blind. She was pretty. She works in a clothing store in Helena. Her age—just right—about 19. A corporal at Helena Aero Tech and I cooked up a foursome. There is not much to do in Helena—three theaters, a few cafes, and two dives (for dancing). We found plenty to do, though. I barely got back to the field at the deadline—2:45 a.m. In my own blundering way, I made another friend. Enough of that.*

*Our academics is now spherical trigonometry. It's plenty deep. It's the type of mathematics needed in celestial navigation (navigation by reference to sun, moon, and stars). With this method, a navigator can locate himself within 15 miles. A heavy bomber travels above cloud disturbances. At times, celestial navigation is the only way for a navigator to make a bombing mission successful.*

*We may not leave as soon as I thought we would. We may be here two weeks yet.*

*Love,*

*Gene*

*February 27, 1943*

*Dear Folks,*

*I am sending some pictures of two models of the B17—the plane I want to be a crew member on. The B17F is my plane. It is one of the latest models. It bristles with guns, it is heavily armored with steel plate, it will fly with half of its engines konked out and with holes in its wings. In short, it is one of the most stable heavy bombers in the world. It is a fortress on wings.*

*I was writing that last letter on my lap sitting on my bunk—an uncomfortable position from every standpoint. I have one of those steel bunks with folding legs. I remember one Saturday night in Jefferson Barracks last summer, we had the same type of bunks. Someone tilted the legs of the bunks of the innocent sleepers at a dangerous angle. All through the night we heard the sounds of collapsing bunks.*

*Don't write until you hear from me again. I'm moving. I don't now where and I can't tell when.*

*Love,*

*Gene*

*March 6, 1943*

*Dear Folks,*

*Thanks for the surprise, Dad. And you're right about navigation. It's a good field of the future.*

*They treat us washouts swell. Last night, about thirty of us were invited to a buffet supper and dance. We had a swell time dancing cheek to cheek. A women's club put the show on. All of the girls were about our age – 18 to 27. For the first time, I saw southern hospitality. All of us cadets agreed that we could have done nothing better on our own.*

*Some jokes, Velma. Did you ever hear about the three guys who wanted a fourth at bridge? One of them cut off one of his arms, and then gangrene set in.*

*I am sending a decent picture of my "wittle self."*

*It seems that I won't get home until I get my wings, if even then. The reason we washouts don't need to stay here long is because we had qualifications for all types of air crew training and had several classifications. We are lucky—only about one of ten pilot washouts is kept in the army as a flying cadet.*

*MY LOCATIONS (in the army):*

*1. Recruiting station at Kansas City, Kansas*

*2. Army Induction and General Classification Center at Fort Leavenworth, Kansas*

*3. Army Air Forces Technical Training Classification and army basic training center at Jefferson Barracks near St. Louis*

*4. Radio Replacement Center for the Eastern States at Patterson Field near Dayton, Ohio*

*5. On duty as radio control tower operator at Air Transport Base at Camp Williams, Wisconsin*

*6. Army Air Forces air crew classification center at Nashville, Tennessee*

*7. Pre-flight school at Maxwell Field near Montgomery, Alabama*

*8. Primary flight training near Helena, Arkansas*

*9. Back to Nashville*

*Of all the places I've been, I probably liked Patterson Field best. Of course, the fact that Patterson Field is near Dayton, Ohio and that one of the swellest girls I've ever known lives in Dayton has something to do with it. She is also very pretty.*

*No, Mom, army camps don't seem like home. Too much is missing.*

*I'll soon be writing from "somewhere else."*

*Love,*

*Gene*

Vee stares at her brother's last line. *Somewhere else* sounds like the place to be. Even though she is only a week into her marriage, she already questions her choices. Home is a thousand miles away, and though she does not like to dwell on negative thoughts, her wedding night proved less romantic than she had imagined it to be. She and Bob are both strong-willed and independent people.

"The hard things we say to each other," she mumbles, thinking back over the week's worth of letters they have exchanged.

She lets the daylight fade to darkness as she waits for Mrs. LaB to return home.

# SEVEN

On Friday morning, Vee wakes with a renewed sense of optimism. She has made a choice to see the fun-loving side of Bob as something they can build upon. And though she misses her family dearly, so many in Caldwell have welcomed her as their own. Her first errand of the day is to order a portrait of Jesus as a gift to the Corns for their generosity. With that done, she stops by to pick up proofs of the wedding photos—her in her pinstriped suit and Bob in his dress uniform. He really is handsome, she thinks.

She swings by the school to walk Betty home from class. Mrs. Corn has dinner ready by five, after which they all gather around the radio to hear Nampa beat Caldwell at basketball 30 to 29. Life is easy and relaxed inside the Corn home until it comes to sports. "We almost swore," Vee recalls as the score had come down to the final point.

To console themselves, Betty pops corn, and the girls shoot darts at a target in a chair.

"Be careful of my upholstery," Mrs. Corn admonishes.

"Don't worry. We haven't hurt the chair."

Vee leans into Betty's ear and whispers, "But look at the wall behind it."

It is good to laugh again in surroundings that feel like home. On some level, she appreciates that Mrs. LaB treats her as an adult, but she still craves the giddiness of childhood and the camaraderie of someone nearer her age.

"Did you bring more letters?"

Vee grabs her purse and removes a bundle as the girls head to the bedroom. Sprawled across the bed, she catches her friend up on the February letters and then pulls out a postcard.

*Ellington Field, Texas*
*March 11, 1943*

> *Arrived here today by rail – came through New Orleans and across ferry at Baton Rouge – saw my first palm trees and Spanish moss.*

> *Gene*

*March 19, 1943*
*Dear Folks,*

> *Here I am in the Lone Star state. I haven't seen any long-horned steers or cowboys, but I have seen a lot of oil wells. The nights are pleasantly cool—a breeze usually blows in from the Gulf.*

> *Our academics are tougher here than in pilot training. We navigators catch hell all the way through. As Claude Ament mentioned, he may become a bombardier and navigator rolled into one. Most navigators are also bombardiers ("bombigators"). The navigator is the most intelligent man on a bomber (as a rule).*

> *Discipline is as tough as it could be here without a class system. I hope I don't catch some tours. I haven't in over a half-year of cadet life. Did I say life? My mistake.*

> *I've been eating like a king the last four months. I weighed in the army at 135 whereas I now weigh around 155.*

> *My pay is still $75 minus minor deductions and pay reservation for war bonds. I get around $45 as cash in hand. I have my shirts and trousers dry cleaned at a cost of from $5 to $10 per month. Meal after meal the food is good. I don't understand it. Army cooks don't usually do such a good job.*

> *Love,*

> *Gene*

*April 3, 1943*

*Dear Folks,*

We changed from wool to cotton uniforms Monday. Thank God. We'll probably have to wear ties regardless of temperature.

I'm taking advantage of some spare time here in the code room. I've passed 12 words receiving and ten words sending—the requirements to be excused from code. Passing is around 8.

This is fun—hear code and not be taking it. When you first start code, you think it will take you. Sometimes it does. I've known two army code operators whose fast code speed came after a nervous breakdown. One of them now can take around 50 words per minute on a signal corps typewriter and talk to someone at the same time.

Our schedule is roughening up. We get up at 5:10 A.M. now. I don't like it, but what can I do? The answer – get up at 5:10 A.M.

*Love,*

*Gene*

*April 8, 1943*

*Dear Folks,*

Sure, I'd be glad to have Velma's picture, but don't send anything elaborate. I've long since learned to cut my equipment to the minimum requirement.

I lead a very dull life—nothing happens to me that would be of interest to anyone else. I did go to Houston last week. The Rice Hotel is a swell place. Officers and cadets really take it over on Saturday night. I am going to get a hotel room one of these times and see how a civilian bed feels.

We get clean barracks (we clean them ourselves), good beds (after you get used to them), and good food. What more can we need? Only one thing. Normal civilian life.

Let's see, by now I have over $200 worth of bonds reserved in the treasury plus being co-owner of several others. I guess I live too much in the future and not enough in the present. After all, some Jap may shorten my future. You know, I sometimes think it's a good thing I enlisted in the army—mentally, I was getting restless. Life was getting dull. Now I have a different kind of dullness to face. It's a change, anyway. Say, I'm going in circles.

*Imuststopas,*

*Gene*

*April 16, 1943*

*Dear Folks,*

    *Tell Hedrick the suit is his. Money? Heck, no. I'll never be able to wear many (if any) of my civilian clothes again anyway. Use any of my clothes you can.*

    *Ament and I located each other here. Small world. It has been that way all through the army. I bump into fellows I know in the most unexpected places and times.*

    *The U.S.O. gives all kinds of shows on the post. About two weeks ago, there were acts here from the Roxy Theatre in New York. One fellow could make all types of sounds; imitate musical instruments, car horns, and so on.*

    *JOKE (labeled so Velma will know) – Major: "The man who sneaked out of the barracks last night and met a girl will please step forward. … Company, Halt!"*

    *We didn't have but two classes today. We've been cleaning barracks. Some generals and other "Big Boys" are coming. There must be something more than a mere general in the air.*

    *Love,*

    *Gene*

*May 1, 1943*

*Dear Folks,*

    *Gad, was I glad to get that fat letter! Mom, I wish I could write such newsy letters as you do. Of course, Velma's writing is variety.*

    *Jack Daly is now a private, first class. He's studying teletype operating. He wants to be an airplane mechanic, and he would be a good one, but the army does funny things. That's one of them.*

    *I had a swell double date this weekend. We danced (rather, I tried), bowled, and went on a picnic. You know, when I get out of the army, I'll probably be able to dance some and bowl fair.*

    *Advanced school or xx (reserve squadron) will be my lot within two weeks. If I do get in, I shall try to get a furlough. There is a chance of a furlough if one has been in the army at least one year with no pass or furlough for one year. In another week, and under the above-stated conditions, I'll be eligible. I never expect much from the army, however.*

    *Love,*

    *Gene*

*May 13, 1943*
*Dear Folks,*

*Oh, Velma, Ruth wrote that you were having some time graduating and all— mostly, all. H'm. I don't doubt it.*

*You'll like this. You can "blurp" and then say, "Pardon my Southern accent."*

*Darn, but my letters are dull. I must be practicing for foreign service, where you can't say anything (almost).*

*I don't think I can get a furlough. I'll probably catch up on my sleep. Anyway, you know I'm still kicking.*

*Love,*
*Gene*

When Vee finishes the letter, she hears slow, heavy breathing and knows Betty has fallen asleep. Carefully, she crawls off the bed and flips off the light on her way out.

Sergeant Corn sits reading alone in the living room. She thanks him again for all his hospitality and walks home in the clear Idaho dark.

***

Bob comes at two the next afternoon. They spend time sorting through the wedding proofs and decide which ones to have reprinted. After clipping their wedding announcement from the paper, they listen to the radio.

Even though he has to return to the dorm for bed check, he comes again at 8:00 the next morning. They walk to the First Baptist Church for Sunday service and communion. For lunch, they stop at Graves restaurant and order steak.

Vee tries to cut a piece. "This is really tough! They must have new cooks."

Bob takes a sample of his own and chews on it for a moment. "And I think this is the old one," he says, pointing to the remainder on his plate.

They talk nonstop through the rest of the meal—Bob about training, Vee about Eugene. As they finish, Bob takes pennies from his pocket and places one under every plate and glass. They hurry to pay and rush out of the restaurant, laughing all the way to the theater.

After the double feature, they wander back to Mrs. LaB's to spend their last hours before Bob will disappear for another week. It has been a good day—reminding Vee why she has made the journey in the first place. At his best, Bob can be loads of fun. She finds it hard to let him leave.

Mrs. LaB must have sensed her mood, because a phone call later, and the Corns appear  asking Vee to evening church with them. It is a good distraction. Tomorrow, she will apply for a job at the dehydrator plant.

# EIGHT

A perpetual night owl, Vee has a habit of staying up past midnight and sleeping until noon. But this Monday morning, she is up at ten. After missing their Saturday hours, she tries a second time to return the wedding proofs only to discover that Stanton's is closed on Mondays.

"We learn every day, don't we?" she says, peering through the store window.

She catches the bus to the Simplot dehydrator plant—a huge complex of long, low buildings covering several acres outside of town. The plant is surrounded by fields of potatoes stretching all the way to the mountains fringing each side of the valley. She finds her way to the office where they hire her on the spot and ask that she start the night shift that evening.

At home, Vee fires off a quick letter to her mother asking that she send her Social Security card. After a late lunch and a long nap, she is up in time to catch *Suspense* with Ida Lupino and Agnes Moorhead on the radio before boarding the bus for the second time that day.

A woman named Suzy logs the time and then takes Vee on a brief tour of the plant. When they step through the door of a massive building with a gracefully arced roof, Vee almost faints. The stench is unbearable. The hanger-like structure—larger than several football fields—is open from wall to wall and supported by five rows of columns running the length of the building.

Suzy waves her hand and shouts over the din of machinery. "It's the largest pile of potatoes in the world!"

There are literally mountains of potatoes, each spud larger than anything Vee's family has grown in their garden at home. Overriding the earthy smell of freshly dug tubers is the unmistakable odor of rot. Vee quickly steps outside the door and vomits.

"Isn't it a thrilling sensation?" Suzy asks when she catches up to her. She lays a sympathetic hand on Vee's shoulder. "If you do manage to stick around, you'll get used to it."

In an equally large but flat-roofed building, Suzy directs Vee to a room with multiple conveyor belts moving row after row of potatoes toward hoppers and lifts, mashers and dryers. Though she can still smell stale potatoes, the building is better ventilated.

"We're going to start you at table 4," Suzy says, motioning toward an empty space beside one of the sections of a conveyor belt. "This is Lois. She'll show you the ropes. When shift is over, come see me again before you leave."

Lois explains the process of specking—digging the eyes from the produce. Before long, Vee finds her rhythm. Only after the first hour does she realize—to her delight—that management has provided a record player to help pass the time. As the work becomes rote, she relaxes into conversation and allows herself to enjoy some music. The hours pass quicker than expected.

She returns home at nine in the morning and falls into bed. At three in the afternoon, she is up long enough to eat something and then goes right back to sleep. At nine-thirty, it is time for work again.

Vee manages to stomach the smell much better her second night. As mundane as the work is, the employees spend time playfully harassing each other until the table supervisors bring them back in line. At one point, Suzy decides to play all of Gene Autry's vocals. Forty-five minutes later, someone throws a potato at her.

"Hey!"

"Why don't you change it up?" someone asks.

For the next thirty minutes, two versions of *Pistol Packin Mama* play on repeat.

***

Vee struggles to adjust her sleep. She hates missing daytime activities like shopping in Boise with Mrs. LaB and visiting the Corns. By the weekend, she is exhausted, and yet that is her time with Bob.

On Saturday, he lets her sleep until three when he comes with mail—a three-dollar wedding gift from his Aunt Opal and a congratulations card from the Vansandts whose son has just enlisted. The couple gives Mrs. Corn the Sollaman's portrait of Jesus. When they return to Mrs. LaB's, they cook a light dinner while Vee rambles on about the new job.

"The fourteen year-old-looking girl across the table from me is eighteen and has been married four months. And the sixteen year-old-looking girl beside her is nineteen and has been married three years!" Vee tries to imagine being married at sixteen. At that age, she had still been running the countryside with her brothers, climbing trees and wading muddy creeks.

Sunday morning, Bob shows up for church, but Vee is too tired to attend. They laze around the house most of the day, listening to the radio and fighting over the dial.

Vee loves all sorts of music, but especially classical. Years earlier, her brother Gene had built his own radio set. Fine-tuning it in their attic bedrooms, he would run the frequencies until his sister would say, "Stop! Let's listen to that." Most often, it would be a concerto or a full-orchestra symphony. Even opera. She loves the Tennessee folk and bluegrass her father plays on his fiddle, but the music is simple—usually built on only three chords. Mozart's complexities draw her in.

When Mrs. LaB returns from a Sunday fitting, the three of them fix dinner. Afterwards, Bob and Vee take the phonograph to the garage and sit in the cold, playing through what records they can find while Mrs. LaB goes to bed. Near curfew, Bob says his goodbyes and wishes his bride a Happy Valentines Day early.

In her room, Vee returns to her brother's letters from the year before.

*Harlingen Army Gunnery School, Texas*
*May 30, 1943*
*Dear Folks,*

*Thanks for the pictures. Gee, would I ever like to be home for a few days! There seems to be no hope. Instead of a furlough, I am here in aerial gunnery school. When they get through with me, I'll be able to do almost any job on a plane.*

*We almost live guns here. We have to be able to take a machine gun apart and put it together again blind-folded. I did it in 33 minutes yesterday. I believe I can cut that time in half in a few days. The idea is to train us so that we can fix a machine gun in the dark. There are times in combat when a light can't be used.*

*We have conventional double-decker army barracks. Food is poor. There are some WAACs here. I might add that they are never unaccompanied wherever they are. They are easy to talk with—they understand army slang.*

*I think we get passes to Mexico next weekend. I'll be a good boy for a change and find some article to bring back and send home.*

*Love,*
*Gene*

*June 7, 1943*
*Dear Folks,*

*I saw Mexico—the worst part, I judge. I went with several other fellows Sunday. We looked over Matamoros, bought some trinkets, had a picture taken, and came back to the USA side about 2 P.M. Living conditions in Matamoros are terrible compared to anything I've ever seen in the US. Matamoros and Brownsville (separated only by the Rio Grande) are as different as night and day.*

*I got a bunch of silver work at the market. Silver goods are hand-worked. Leather goods are beautiful, too. They put a high lustre on silver by beating it. By spinning it, it has a dull lustre.*

*We could use American money so long as it was $2 bills or silver. We were glad to come back across the Rio Grande. In short, we were glad to get back in the USA.*

*Gene*


*Ground Range, HAGS, Texas*
*June 17, 1943*
*Dear Folks,*

*We moved out here to the ground range on the 11th. It's about two miles from the Gulf. This living among rattlesnakes, wild hogs, coral snakes, spiders of every description, wolves, bob-cats, and mosquitoes is foreign service to many of us.*

*I'm almost "NUTS" from firing guns. I fired rifles at moving targets this morning until my arms ached. We've been firing .50 caliber machine guns the last three days that sound like automatic canons.*

*So Velma's engaged? H'm. That's the way it goes.*

*About what to send me—it's this way. I really need nothing except a two-month furlough ... that I can't get. A furlough could do big things for my morale, though.*

*Love,*
*Gene*


*HAGS, Texas*
*June 27, 1943*
*Dear Folks,*

*Thanks for the news and the cards. And the birthday present – you shouldn't ha' done it.*

*We moved back to the field Friday night. We flew yesterday and today. I have four runs completed so far. All of our daylight hours are used by the army—in other words, we're busy hurrying and waiting.*

*Texas looks good from the air. We fire out over the Gulf. Our bomber is the A29 or AT18. I enjoy the trip over the Gulf in the A29. It's so smooth. The Mae Wests we wear are to keep us afloat in case we have to pull silk over the Gulf. Mae Wests are life preservers inflated with either CO2 or air.*

*One of my fellow cadets, Fred Hench, acquired a new name today – "the mushroom kid." While putting one of his parachute straps in the proper position, he accidentally pulled the ripcord. You know the answer. Silk all over the ramp. A WAAC on duty in the parachute room said, "It happens in the best of families."*

*Love,*

*Gene*

At one in the morning, Vee can no longer keep her eyes open, so she crawls into bed and sleeps until late Monday afternoon. She has been tasked with buying a box of candy and a Valentine's Day card for the table supervisor. She picks up a few extra cards for family and then accompanies Mrs. Corn to the hospital to deliver cookies to a young boy recovering from an illness.

"Whoever named you *Joy* sure knew what they were doing," Vee tells Mrs. Corn. "You seem to spread it everywhere."

Mrs. Corn takes the compliment in stride and delivers Vee back to her temporary home.

The mailbox is stuffed with letters from Missouri including her Social Security card. A letter from the state of Idaho includes her marriage license. Though she may not feel it yet, the government now considers her officially an adult.

Equipment problems at the plant complicate Vee's continued struggle to adjust to the night shift. But what bothers her the most is Gene's latest letter forwarded from her mom.

*Mac Dill Field, Florida*

*February 14, 1944*

*Dear Folks,*

*This will be a long letter. Get ready for anything. This may be the last letter I write for a long time. We are definitely being toughened up for the "kill or be killed."*

*I should have a power of magistrate attached to that power of attorney to be sure it is good anywhere, but I didn't (and won't) have time. By proper legal procedure, you may insure its legality later—if necessary.*

*This letter may seem rash. But war is rash. We have to get that way. Don't be surprised from where or from when my next letter reaches you. I may be here. I may be there. I may be home or I may not be home before I arrive "there." Don't worry about anything. No news is definitely good news. Remember that even if I sound and act rough I don't mean it deep down as this letter would indicate. I had better shock you a little now in preparation.*

*If my letters are meaningless from now on, understand it is for the best. War is a rough game.*

*I can't tell you where we're going from here even though I do know. I may move several times between letters. More and more my letters will tell nothing but personal affairs and ideas. Most of the time you won't have any idea where I am or what I am doing, but bet on this—it'll be to end Japanazis. In short, to end this damned war.*

*Now to answering your questions and to the lighter side of life. That Spanish girl, ah! I very definitely have been with her several times, and I like her a lot. Her name— (Connie) Carmen del Llano. Description—5'2" tall, properly proportioned, around twenty, pretty face, cute freckles, (that's not all). She is one of the sweetest, most understanding girls I have ever known. She doesn't drink or smoke. Around here, that's something. I've met her family. One brother (she has three brothers and no sisters) is overseas and has been for over a year. The other brothers are going to high school. Her mother and father can speak only a few words of English. They treat me swell. Connie herself speaks perfect English and Spanish along with some German. That makes me ashamed of my poor use of only one language.*

*I've met a lot of feminine people here—all kinds. One, a part-time model, a beautiful blonde. She is very popular, needless to say. Another, a brunette, "been around" too much for me if you get what I mean. She's off my list.*

*But Connie—there's the one. I could fall in love with a girl like her so easy.*

*I got a lot off my chest this time. Maybe this is a decent letter for a change.*

*Love,*

*Gene*

Her brother is in love. It should be a bright spot in her week, but the tone of the rest of the letter disturbs her greatly. For the first time since the war started, Vee is afraid for one of her own.

# NINE

**Vee's life now arranges itself into three neat categories— work, evenings with the Corns, and weekends with Bob.**

Her husband spends most of Saturdays and Sundays hanging out at Mrs. LaB's, listening to the radio or helping Vee add clippings and photos to their scrapbook. If Vee is not too tired, they attend church. Occasionally, Bob offers to cook.

"Dear Diary, Bob cooked pork chops for supper. No comment."

"Dear Diary, Bob cooked the remainder of the pork chops for dinner. Still no comment."

The Corns continue to treat Vee as family. She attends Betty's school concerts, enjoys occasional parties in their home, and makes sure Betty is caught up on all the news about Gene.

Work at the plant is tedious but not difficult once Vee acclimates to the smell. The line crew plays records at full volume. At lunch and during breaks, someone occasionally pounds out a few songs on a the poorly-tuned piano in the break room. Though it is challenging to keep workers, the ones who stay manage to push a few boundaries, bringing a little fun to the long nights. That is, until management hires a new table supervisor.

"Ladies! You need to pipe down and concentrate on your work."

The women along the line tip their heads and eye each other quietly until she passes, and then Toni lets out a loud "Waa-hoo!"

On another night, the supervisor catches Vee and Lois laughing too loudly over some anecdote.

"I have to move one of you. You're talking a constant stream."

The girls stay put as Lois replies, "Then we'll have to talk a constant scream!"

Management keeps restrictions to a minimum, hoping the women on the line will stay, but apparently the new table lady has not gotten the memo. One evening, she parks herself repeatedly between Vee and Ruth, and finally says, "If you can't stop talking, I'll have to move one of you."

Ruth returns the challenge. "If you do, I won't stay."

Despite the relaxed camaraderie, when the supervisor asks Vee to change positions and lift heavy trays for the evening, she cries, "Anything but specking!"

The constant threat of losing employees makes for few consequences when any of the women are late or miss a shift. One night, Vee's alarm goes off, but after she shuts it down, she accidentally falls back to sleep. The next evening, the supervisor asks where she had been the night before.

"I missed the bus, I think."

"You just think, huh? You aren't sure?"

Vee rolls her eyes. "Well, I was asleep at the time."

She also finds it convenient to miss work on the rare occasions when Bob scores an overnight pass.

Even as her routine settles in, she finds comfort in sharing Eugene's letters with Betty.

*Ellington Field, Texas*
*July 4, 1943*
*Dear Folks,*

I'm a private first class now instead of a buck private. I'll get a light pay hike. I did good enough in tower school to receive a promotion. Most of my study now is control tower. I take some code yet.

We got our air member wings (and graduated as aerial gunners) today. And here we are back at Ellington Field. Coming back here to the food as it is served is like landing in heaven.

We probably go to advanced from here. We will parade in Houston tomorrow. I can almost feel the sweat running down my back.

H'm, Velma, some trash eh? If you made up that dishwater story, it is good, for you, considering your low ebb of mentality. Ho! Ho! Ho! Ho! Oops – there went my false teeth.

Love,

Gene

*San Marcos Army Air Field, Texas*
*July 17, 1943*
*Dear Folks,*

We arrived here yesterday. I can see we are going to be so busy that sleep will be incidental—a luxury in one sense of the word. Inspections are going to be rough. The ramp (where tours are walked) will be the most popular place on the post. Did I say popular? I should have said unpopular.

We have classes tomorrow—night school also for the next two weeks at least.

I'm sending a picture of myself as an H.G. (hot gunner). It shows what the well-dressed aerial gunner will wear.

We have been busy from 6:30 A.M. to 10:15 P.M. every day. We have classes from 8 A.M. to 10 P.M. We study navigational stars at night the last few minutes of each class day. We will have to learn about a hundred first magnitude stars.

For dead reckoning computation, we use a vector computer and slide rule combination known as the E6B. It's wonderful. A twist of the wrist and there's the answer. My following sentence should probably be censored – the E6B will do everything for you a woman will except one, and it'll do that on an examination.

*We were issued hack watches a few days ago. A hack watch is an accurate watch whose variation from the second is known – in other words, time to the second.*

*Love,*

*Gene*

*August 3 1943*

*Dear Folks,*

*We started flying last week, and what did I do but get airsick for the first time. I wasn't the only one and how. On our next flight mission we swing the compass (a method of finding compass deviation). On a "swing the compass" mission, even pilots who are used to flying every day get airsick. There is more airsickness and more accidents in navigation training than any other air crew training because the flights are so long.*

*We got the results of some of our ground missions today. Log procedure seems to be all important. Oh, my aching head! My grade was 50. So far as I can find, there were none over 60. Yet, some fellows get through this.*

*This is the worst drag I've ever had in my life. We even fly this weekend, Saturday evening until 7 P.M. Then we will be too tired to enjoy open post if we even get it. I guess they are breaking us in for what is ahead. In foreign service, the navigator is usually the mess officer and tactical officer, or so they say, in addition to being the hardest-working member of the air crew.*

*Did I ever tell you about my first DR mission? I was doing pilotage navigation in the co-pilot's seat. My log accidentally blew out the window. No log – no grade. And you know, I had the darnedest time making everyone believe my log blew out accidentally. Oh, well. Times are tough all over.*

*I better stop. Old Man Time is punching me with his pitchfork.*

*Love,*

*Gene*

*August 29, 1943*

*Dear Folks,*

*Was Velma ever on the beam! What a mass of letter. Why can't I run on like that?*

*Yesterday was my unlucky day. I walked my first tours since I have been a cadet. Our officers are getting rough. Gigs just add up. Then the guys in the orderly room add two* and two and get ten. I had only two tours, but I was posted for six. I finally got the mess straightened out and walked my two tours.

They are grinding the washing machine—several fellows have washed. We are all treading unsteady ground because of the new grading system. We only have about two weeks and two months to go, and they keep getting rougher on us. Will I ever be glad when I can really relax again.

We may have some flights that will take us over Missouri. If I can get close to Harrisonville, I would be tempted to bail out at the proper moment. Yep.

Mom, you can really write newsy letters. I just don't have anything to write that I could call news. A lot of stuff that might be interesting is military information, so "mum" is the word. Like at gunnery school where we were using the Sperry automatic computing gun sight which was a secret to the public until rather recently. That gun sight, properly used, is a charm. It increases the lethal density (killing range) of a .50 calibre Browning machine gun to twice that obtained by using any other type of gunsight.

The army has a way of taking all the fun out of anything. I'm just wondering how long it will be before a navigator does every job on a bomber.

Love,

Gene


San Marcos, Texas

September 18, 1943

Dear Folks,

Guess where I'm writing this from—the U.S.O. at San Marcos and on Saturday night, and with dancing going on in the next room. The percentage (girl to boy) is bad. Free stationery. So, a letter. In short, things are dull.

A tropical storm has been passing through Texas. So far, we haven't got any of it. All of the planes have been flown to other fields. If the planes had been here, we would probably not have had a free weekend.

I am out "stag" tonight. On the whole, unsatisfactory. Right now I'm waiting to cut in on somebody when the right music hits me. Cutting in is the only way to get to dance. So far, I've had one full dance. Oh, well, times are rough all over.

Love,

Gene

*September 27, 1943*

*Dear Folks,*

*If things go on as they have the last three days, I may wash out and have plenty of time. We were so busy this weekend, I didn't even leave the post. Many times have I wished I had asked for bombardier training instead of this. It's easier and shorter. I don't think they give cadets a third chance in the air crew in officer training. If the army knows what is best, they'll make an officer out of me, having spent this much time, money, and experience on me. Maybe I'll get through this yet (if luck is with me). Things have looked dark in the past and I'm still here. I better stop this.*

*Love,*

*Gene*

# TEN

**February 29th is a Tuesday.** The girls at work make leap year jokes. Late in the morning, when everyone's feet are aching, Lois says, "Speaking of leaping, aren't spiders fortunate to have so many legs to stand on?" They all agree it would be an advantage.

"Hey, Vee!" Ruth calls from down the line. "Do you have wolves back home in Missouri?"

"Galore!" she tells them.

Ruth smiles a rye smile. "They're here, too. In fact, Evelyn married one of them."

Everyone but Evelyn laughs. "Let's get to work," she says. "Our country needs us!"

On the weekend, Bob shows up with a severe sore throat. Vee plays nursemaid while he sleeps most of the weekend. With nothing else to do, she pulls out the last packet of Gene's old letters.

*San Marcos Army Air Field, Texas*
*October 10, 1943*
*Dear Folks,*

*Four more flights to go. I am doing better in celestial navigation then I did in DR, thank God. I've traveled about 4000 miles the last six days with three 8 or 9-hour flights. My element has flown twice to Wichita, Kansas and once to Walnut Ridge, Arkansas. I was closer to home than I've been for ages. On my first trip to Wichita, our plane developed electrical troubles on the return trip. We landed at Tinker Field near Oklahoma City and got passes to the city while the plane was being repaired. Those civilian beds in the Biltmore Hotel really were all right.*

*Either this weekend or the next, I shall order my officer's clothing. I can see the bill now—about $300. I think I'll make the grade in navigation. My trouble is that I work to learn to navigate instead of to make grades. I can't be certain about anything until they pin the bars and wings on me.*

*Love,*
*Gene*

*October 18, 1943*
*Dear Folks,*

*It is possible that I may be home for Thanksgiving, though probably before. We finish in about three weeks. I have ordered my uniform. It is going to be snazzy, I can see.*

*We were issued a new celestial navigation kit last week. Kit makes it sound small. All of it weighed about thirty pounds. We got new Elgin hack watches. I got a Link sextant. I like it better than any other sextant I've ever used.*

*I believe the only thing that could ever wash me now is a stroke of bad luck. I practically have that gold bar and those navigator wings in my hands now—so close and yet so far.*

*Time goes fast. I better sign off.*
*Love,*
*Gene*

*October 24, 1943*

*Dear Folks,*

    *I don't know when we graduate now. The army has changed it again. Now I can't be sure of getting home. Some of the fellows in the class before us went directly to bombardier training or operational training.*

    *We have been going to school on Sunday lately. Yes, when we should be resting or sleeping. The navigator works for hours before the flight. Then after the flight, the pilot, co-pilot, bombardier, crew chief, radio operator, and gunners are free. The navigator reports to the intelligence office with the history of the flight. God only knows when he may be free.*

    *We graduate the 13th. I wish you could be here to pin my navigator wings on, but I know you can't. I am still hoping I can get home.*

    *I heard Pistol-Packin' Mama was on the Hit Parade.*

*Love,*

*Gene*

*Rapid City Air Field, South Dakota*

*November 26, 1943*

    *Arrived Rapid City the 24th. Slept nine hours last night after no sleep the night before. I'll give you an exact address later.*

*Gene*

*November 28, 1943*

*Dear Folks,*

    *I've been on the post three days and flown two of them. We are even busier than ever. We are flying B17 Fs and B17 Gs with chin turrets. It's the first time I ever used throat mikes.*

    *In a way, it is swell being an officer. We get good quarters and good food. Officers Club dues here are only $3 a month. One thing here is rough—officers are fined $75 (one-half base pay) if they are not where they are scheduled to be. Uniform regulations are strict too.*

    *I got five shots all at once yesterday. Two more shot sessions and we have all our overseas shots.*

    *I won't give you my address because it is supposed to change again very soon.*

*Love,*

*Gene*

*Mac Dill Field, Tampa, Florida*
*December 6, 1943*
*Dear Folks,*

*Moved again—to a warmer climate. My barracks are right on the bay. It is actually too warm for comfort here during the day. I don't know how long we will be here or how long we will be in the US, but not long.*

*Love,*
*Gene*

*December 18, 1943*
*Dear Folks,*

*Yes, I did have a turkey dinner in Rapid City on Thanksgiving Day. And I may have been mad when that picture was taken. The army always picks out the most unusual times to take pictures.*

*I am not getting any bonds for November or December and maybe not for January. I want to get on my feet financially first. Being an officer takes money. $150 flying pay this month will help.*

*I agree with you, Mom, on Sinatra. I wonder if he's really "heart-broken" because the army didn't take him. Here is a common statement, "The navy gets the pay, the marines get the glory, and the army does the work."*

*Christmas shopping, for me, is almost impossible. I'll send you a twenty. You use it as you see fit.*

*Merry Christmas,*
*Gene*

Vee returns the letters to the box. She feels melancholy in having finished them again. Gene is still stationed at Mac Dill in Florida, but she knows that could change at any moment. He managed a brief furlough to visit his family before going on to Rapid City, but it now seems as if Vee will not see him again until the war was over. She can only guess when that might be.

She wakes her husband and sends him back to the dorms, back to his own uncertain future.

# ELEVEN

**The pace in Caldwell runs similar to Vee's hometown of Harrisonville, Missouri.** Both small towns survive on small businesses and by supporting the local farming industries. But in Caldwell, farming means thousand-acre productions as opposed to the hundred-acre farms she grew up around.

Caldwell also supports a small community college. Successful in the past, things looked dire for enrollment during the early war years until the military stepped in with its 311th Training Detachment—the program Bob is enrolled in. His training will prepare him for the air, as the college substitutes military studies for some of the more academic rigors.

As for big-city shopping, Boise cannot compare to Kansas City—a mere 26,000 residents to Kansas City's 400,000. Still, she escapes to Boise with Mrs. LaB as often as she can. Now that she is a working girl, she has money to burn.

"My income tax for last year was $47!" Ruth complains one night. "I was going to save out of my last two checks, but...." She smiles devilishly. "I went to town and found the cutest pair of midriff pajamas, the darlingest skirt, and the sweetest white blouse. So what do you suppose happened?"

"What about your income tax?"

"Oh, Mother would rather pay it than see her little ole baby daughter go to jail."

"Have you talked to her about it yet?"

"Nope, but I will. I always speak to her on money matters. In fact, that's about the only time I speak to her."

After paying her rent, Vee manages to pick up a few new clothes for herself. She is proud of her figure and eager to show it off in the latest fashion. The idea of saving for a rainy day does not occur to her.

Letters continue to arrive from home. One afternoon, Vee receives a package from Gene with a photo of him in his Second Lieutenant uniform. She shares it and two letters with Betty.

"He really is a hunk," Betty says, staring at the picture.

"You're gonna hate this," Vee warns. "He sent Mom the addresses of six girls he wants to stay in touch with. SIX! And I thought he was in love with one named Carmen." She opens an envelope and shows her friend the list before starting to read.

> *Hunter Field, Georgia*
> *March 3, 1944*
> *Dear Folks,*
>
> *We flew here two days ago. We won't be here long. I don't believe we will get leaves. We are getting some time to ourselves. Rest and sleep are wonderful, as are these nights in Savannah.*
>
> *Would you save the list for me? I can't remember too many numbers, and paper can be lost. There are some swell girls on the list, girls a fellow likes to see again.*
>
> *All of us officers of my crew are in the same room. The pilots stayed here last night. They put a bottle of hair tonic in my bed, tying the cap to the foot. When I took the bottle*

*out, hair tonic was spread from the foot to the head of my bed. I was so tired, into bed I*
*went, hair tonic or no hair tonic.*

    *That's all, folks,*

    *Gene*

Betty presses her chin into her hands. "Maybe you should send him a picture of me and tell him how smart I am."

"Wouldn't that be wonderful?" Vee knows Betty will not check off all of Gene's boxes, but she does not want to hurt her feelings. Instead, she shows her the next letter. "Look at the header!"

*South of the Equator*
*March 11, 1944*
*Dear Folks,*

    *I don't think I should tell where I am anymore than I already have. Our weather is*
*definitely mucky. The sun really bears down.*

    *We have covered a lot of land and water the last few days. We have a lot more*
*to cover. I have been doing OK in navigation. My ETAs average from 10 seconds to 3*
*minutes off. My course has never been over 6 miles off. We fly automatic pilot most of the*
*time and it is really swell. Steady as a rock.*

    *During the last few weeks in the States, I got some stick time in our new plane. It's*
*a lot different from a PT-19.*

    *I don't think the censor will clip any of this. My pen is packed away. I may be able*
*to tell all about this trip when I get to my final destination.*

    *Love,*

    *Gene*

    *P.S.: If anything ever happens to me, would you write to Carmen and tell her?*
*Thanks. As things stand, only you would be notified.*

"I knew it!" Vee says as she folds the letter. "He's really in love with this one."

The girls finish their sodas and walk home. After dinner, they attend a Tuesday night youth service where nearly twenty children, ages six to twenty, come forward to dedicate their lives to Jesus.

The bus arrives at 9:30. Several of her coworkers are absent. Two had gone to a dance and have not shown up.

"Where are your pals?"

Vee keeps quiet. She knows the girls are good at making up their own excuses.

"The bus missed Wilma," someone says.

"Translation: Wilma missed the bus!"

"And nobody's seen Virginia for days. Wonder what's up."

When they are all scolded again for talking too much, Vee does not say over five sentences the rest of the night. At break she complains to Ruth. "I can't keep my friends. They keep getting moved." She nibbles at a piece of cake. "Being such a quiet child, I forced myself to talk, and I suppose I overdid it."

Ruth rolls her eyes. "It's the only thing that keeps me working here. If we couldn't carry on, I'd be out of here tomorrow. But do be careful. Several women got their walking papers yesterday. Evelyn probably got fired because she smelled like she'd had a pint."

Vee lets out a long breath. "I wondered where everyone was."

In the morning, she answers several letters before going to bed and then finishes out the week in quiet servitude at the plant. On Friday, cousin Lee picks her up. They stop by the college to check on Bob. His tonsillitis has worsened, and he is spending a few days at the Gowen Field Hospital.

By mid-week, Vee has come down with Bob's sore throat.

"My days are numbered," she moans as Mrs. LaB spoons hot soup into her mouth. "I think I'm going to die."

"Nonsense. Just stay home and get well. They can do without you tonight."

Vee wonders if she can get by missing another night so soon after missing the bus twice in two weeks. She takes solace in the fact that she is a good worker—when she's there.

She pushes herself to work the next evening even though her throat is still sore. As soon as she arrives, her bosses called her on the carpet for making the bus wait ten minutes. They have little sympathy for her illness.

On the line, the girls strike up their usual banter, trying their best not to let it get out of hand.

"Yesterday was my one-year anniversary," Vee announces. "One year ago, Bob and I had our first date. Fried popcorn, brewed coffee. *Dearly Beloved* on the radio."

"Well *that* sounds romantic!" Ruth jokes.

"Maybe it was," Vee says, keeping the rest of her thoughts to herself. To change the subject, she asks, "How is it coming with your income tax?"

"Oh! Swell! I had to fast talk the front office into not making me pay it twice! And now I owe the $45 I borrowed to the Red Cross."

\*\*\*

On March 18th, Vee checks the mailbox to find it empty. It has been a week since anyone has heard from Gene, but she remembers his admonition, *No news is good news.*

It is three days later when an airmail letter arrives from their mom. Vee reads the letter three times and then the accompanying Western Union telegram before she allows the panic to set in.

*Washington DC 133 pm 3/18*
*Truman Trucil Hammontree. Harrisonville, Mo*
  *The secretary of war desires me to express his deep regret that your son Second Lieut Eugene L Hammontree has been reported missing since Fourteen March between American area and North African areas. Letter follows.*
  *Ulio*
  *The Adjutant General*

He is only listed as missing, she keeps telling herself. The circumstances could be anything. There is always hope.

The news triggers something else in Vee—something from her past. She does not remember her biological mother. She was barely three and a half when her mother died of appendicitis. Too young to fully process the loss, a young Vee had held it somewhere deep within that her mother would simply appear one day, even though her father had remarried. Vee's step-mom, the one who raised her, is a kind and caring woman who fills her step-children's lives with as much love as anyone can want. But that pall, that nagging feeling that things can change in an instant is ever present, always acting as a subtle barrier that keeps most others at bay. The exception is Eugene.

Vee cries herself to sleep.

# TWELVE

**The next few nights at work pass agonizingly slow.** Vee hopes the job will keep her mind off of gruesome things, but little seems to help. When one of the girls plays *The Air Corps Song*, Vee loses her temper and yells for them to turn it off.

The days are no better. She waits for a letter from her mom or someone, anyone, who can give her news about her brother. When none arrives, she goes back to bed until time for work. At last, her mother forwards a second telegram. Vee's hands shake as she opens it.

*Washington DC 305 pm 3/22*

*Truman Trucil Hammontree. Harrisonville, Mo*

    *Am pleased to inform you report received states your son Second Lieut Eugene L Hammontree who was previously reported missing has returned to military control. Report further states he was hospitalized for observation and treatment of minor injuries. Undoubtedly he will communicate with you at an early date concerning his welfare and whereabouts.*

    *Ulio*

    *The Adjutant General*

Included in the envelope are two letters—one from her mom, and a brief one from Eugene himself. She goes right to Gene's.

*Postmaster, Miami, Florida*
*March 21, 1944*
*Dear Folks,*

*I can not even give my approximate geographical location. There has been a change of plan. We have been taking life very easy the last several days. I am going to get fat at this rate. Food is good. I am all right. Don't worry when I don't write or when mail I do write is delayed.*

*Love,*
*Gene*

Vee lets out a squeal of excitement. Her brother is fine, even making light of his situation. It is all she needs to bring her out of her recent stupor. She faces work with a renewed sense of optimism.

***

Specking is a dull and repetitious activity that requires little thought. Occasionally, someone cuts themselves, but for the most part, the job is hardest on the hand and arm muscles—gripping potatoes and carving out eye after eye.

"Twenty years from now, we'll all have rheumatism and wonder where we got it."

Lois pipes up. "If we keep working here, we won't live twenty years." She adds, "I'm not feeling too well tonight, as it is."

"The nurse can fix you up. Don't tell her what ails you, though. If you have a headache, the stomach ache, a cold, or gas, she'll give you a little white capsule. So, just ask for a little white capsule."

"Say, where's Angie tonight?" someone asks.

"Oh, she's in another conference with the bosses. Three nights of conference with all of the supervisors. Must be really dull in there."

"*Talk with Table-Ladies.* A play in three acts."

Just then, Angie steps up behind Lois.

"Boo! You're talking!"

Lois nearly jumps out of her skin. When she calms down, she says, "Well, now, if you hadn't told us, we never would have known."

"This is Angie," Vee tells the new girl across the table. "She's our chaperon. She sees to it that we all behave like ladies."

A redhead at the other end of the table shouts, "Angie, if you don't make Ruth stop throwing *pa tay toes* at me, I'm going to climb over there and beat the heck out of her!"

Vee winks at the new girl. "Well, she tries, anyway."

Sunday school with Bob is one of the highlights of her week. During one class, Mrs. Bourland gives a true/false questionnaire. Vee passes at 60 percent, but Bob scores an impressive 92. *He's a smart man, he keeps telling hisself,* Vee thinks, and smiles at her own joke.

Family correspondence fills her mailbox again.

*Somewhere in Brazil*
*March 25, 1944*
*Dear Folks,*

*Here I am taking life easy as yet. I am in the head-quarters building waiting for the pilot. I thought I had just as well do some writing, having read all available magazines. This tropical weather gets me down. It's so hard to get good sound sleep. I wake up every two or three hours in a pool of sweat. A fellow sunburns in no time.*

*I've been eating plenty of tropical fruits, especially bananas. They keep me "regular." I had better stop.*

*Love,*
*Gene*


*Somewhere in Brazil*
*March 29, 1944*
*Dear Folks,*

*We are still waiting for something to happen since our previous plans were changed*

*in a way I am unable to write. We get plenty of rest and food. We have movies outside
(when it is not raining). We can get Cokes and ice cream part of the time.*

*I can understand some few words of the natives here. Natives take care of our rooms.
I take a rest—nap, if possible—about noon. If I come back in an hour, the bed is made
up again. Our quarters are actually better than any of the best hotels here.*

*We have a good radio in the officers lounge. We get good rebroadcast programs.*

*Remember, if anything happens to me, tell Carmen. Thanks.*

*I must stop this with love,*

*Gene*

In addition to Gene's letters, the week's excitement centers on Mrs.
LaB's new telephone. It takes a round or two with the man who installs it,
but as soon as it is operational, Bob calls.

"How did you know Mrs. LaB got a phone?"

"Intuition."

"Sure. I bet Betty told you."

They make plans to visit cousin Lee over the weekend. He brings them
to Aunt Annie's just in time for lunch—spare ribs, wieners and sauerkraut,
mashed potatoes, asparagus, beet pickles, tea, fruit cake, doughnuts,
peaches, green beans, and cherry pie! In the afternoon, they carry freshly
popped corn around as they inspect the gardens, and then Lee and Bob
decide to fish. For their evening meal, Annie prepares chili and pears, and
fills them up with more fruit cake, doughnuts, and cherry pie. As a belated
wedding gift, she gives them a bath towel and sends them home with a
variety of home-canned goods.

Back in Vee's room, Bob brakes the news that he is being transferred
to Luke Field in California.

"California? And just as this was beginning to feel like home."

"You could follow me there," he suggests.

She remembers how many times Gene has been shipped all over the
country. "I would just get a new job, and you'd be gone again."

Her comment sparks an argument that lasts several minutes. She sends Bob back to the dorms with the disagreement unresolved.

***

The morning's mail includes a long-overdue letter from Vee's best friend, Jeanie, and a lovely note from Carmen del Llano, the girl Gene seems most enamored with. Her handwriting flows into a beautiful script, and her English is flawless—something that should not surprise Vee, but does. Carmen writes about Gene as if she has known him all her life. Vee likes her immediately.

She spends an hour writing return letters and, with pen still in hand, writes a brief resignation letter to Angie at the plant. There is something thrilling in the act, so she takes her latest paycheck and shops for a new Easter dress and shoes. She catches Betty after school and learns that the entire Corn family is taking a vacation to Santa Ana, California.

"Wow," Vee says, thinking it over. "California seems the place to be right now."

"I wish you could go, too. Maybe you'd really like it and want to move there. You know, be where Bob is."

"But he probably won't be there long." She does not voice her other concern—that perhaps her marriage is a mistake. As much fun as she and Bob have, they spend an equal amount of time bickering. The more they learn of each other, the less they find in common.

The next night, Bob manages to keep the dorm key with him as he lays beneath the covers for bed check. A few minutes later, he shows up at Mrs. LaB's until four in the morning.

"They're having a party for us boys before we ship out. You should come."

"I think I have food poisoning," she complains, excusing herself from the festivities. She really does feel awful. Her wistfulness is compounded by the fact that Betty and her family are now out of town.

Vee sleeps through the next day and night, but feels better the morning of Easter service. She dresses in her new outfit and puts on the lovely corsage Bob gave her the day before. When he shows up, he is driving a little green Ford!

"Get in!" he calls, holding something in his hand. "I have FOUR gas stamps!"

He drives them past the church and out of town toward Nampa. Vee sees what looks like the entire town dressed in their Easter best and wishes she could see more of them at church. But Bob drives on to Boise and then into the mountains. He navigates the slopes until they are high above the valley, looking out across the plain. It is stunning—clear and crisp, the towns just postage stamps below. On their return, they buy food for a picnic by the Boise River.

After lunch, Bob lets Vee drive. He directs her through Middleton and Notis and Parma. Late in the evening, they stop to picnic in a cemetery and explore the river before dark. After dark, they make love in the car as the full moon rises bright in the sky.

# THIRTEEN

*Somewhere in North Africa*
*April 5, 1944*
*Dear Folks,*

 *Back to the old APO number. I don't know for how long. The co-pilot and I are always fighting, mildly of course. We go around and around and where we stop nobody knows. That's the reason my writing is so jagged. I better stop this and rest—so much work to wrestle and write at the same time.*

 *Love,*
 *Gene*

Vee sorts the postcard into place and pulls out two letters dated April 9th—one from Gene and one from Wayne.

*Somewhere in Italy*

*April 9, 1944*

*Dear Folks,*

*I have a fourth APO now as you see. I probably won't get any mail for ages. I haven't received any now for over five weeks. I've had too many APO changes.*

*From what I could find out here, the War Department told you more about me than I thought I could. Maybe I censor my mail too strictly. I have one consolation—the enemy can gain nothing from my mail. The trouble is, neither can anyone else.*

*This is Easter Sunday back there in the States. To us it's another day—we hope a day closer to setting our feet on the good old USA. Nothing like it. Luxuries galore.*

*Love,*

*Gene*

*APO Postmaster*

*April 9, 1944*

*Dear Velma,*

*The folks said that Eugene had been missing since the fourteenth of March, but I got a letter from them and they said he had been found and just had minor injuries. I am glad he is alright. I hope Bob is alright by this time and going strong again.*

*You asked me to tell you all about England so I will try. To my notion it is a heck of a poor place. It is cloudy and rainy most of the time. Maybe someday I will get back and then I can tell what all I did while I was over here.*

*You said I had a sister that thinks an awful lot of me. She is the most wonderful girl in all this world. I wish I could be back home and have some of the good times we all used to have together. But I guess that will have to wait.*

*I am glad you like your job. What kind of work do you do?*

*I liked to laughed my head off when I read the jokes you told.*

*Well, I will close. Write soon.*

*Love as ever,*

*Wayne*

*Somewhere in Italy*
*April 12, 1944*
*Dear Folks,*

    *My first mail arrived today—your V mail letter dated March 22.*

    *I can tell you something about our accident now that we are at our destination. We "ditched" our plane crossing the Atlantic. To airmen, ditching is landing a land plane in water in a dire emergency. As you know, land planes don't have much in the line of floating qualities.*

    *We were lucky. All of us got out with our skins. Most of us received only minor injuries. We had two nights on a raft—incidentally, they're wonderful, couldn't do without them. A navy destroyer picked us up.*

    *The bombardier is still in the hospital. The rest of us got out in about a week. All I have to show is a scar or two.*

    *There is a German radio station we get quite a kick out of—something of humor even in war. One program in English is a killer called "Axis Sally"—music we are used to but played by Germans, news (of course, pro-German), and other odds and ends. They sign off something like this, "Good luck to you Yankees and a sweet kiss from Axis Sally." Then the song "I'm a Yankee Doodle Dandy" follows. Then silence.*

    *Then love,*

    *Gene*

*April 20, 1944*
*Dear Folks,*

    *I'm at the Officers' Club with free stationery and pen and plenty of light so here we go.*

    *By the way, would you send me Mary Griffin's address? I owe her at least a thank you note. She treated me swell while I was there—Savannah.*

    *I'm writing to Carmen, too. Our song "Stardust" was just played on the piano. Some Italian musicians are playing classical music now—good deal. This is better than going mad back on the field as a person is prone to do if he stays there all the time.*

    *Love,*

    *Gene*

*April 21, 1944*

*Dear Folks,*

    *This is just a note. Thanks for telling Carmen about those telegrams. I saw her almost every spare moment I had after I first met her. You know I mentioned that I could fall I love with a girl like her. Well, I did. She is really swell.*

    *Love,*

    *Gene*

"I told you, didn't I?" Vee says to Bob one night. "Carmen is the one. Betty will be heart-broken."

Unsure when he will ship out, Bob visits every evening that he can. He and Vee play cards, watch movies, and eat at their regular haunt—Cheesbroughs. Bob's younger brother Ed is graduating high school, so they put together a gift package to send home.

Vee listens to the radio every spare moment—caught up in the music and often forgetting her chores. And always, she writes letters home.

One day, an APO letter arrives addressed directly to her, *Mrs. Robert Beckerdite*. She hurries to tear it open.

*Somewhere in Italy*

*April 18, 1944*

*Dear Velma and Bob,*

    *I'm several thousand miles from the USA now—too far. We have been here several weeks. As you know, I've had one close call before even getting here. I've been lucky so far. Luck has more connection with flying than most people know.*

    *There is a German radio station that features "Axis Sally." Instead of under-mining our morale, as intended, they build it up. We know their claims are false. I don't see why they waste power on the station.*

    *Velma, what kind of work do you do? Give me the lowdown.*

    *Love,*

    *Gene*

Betty sends a postcard from California gushing about "sailors, marines, and everything!" They are eating huge breakfasts, bowling and swimming, have visited Chinatown and Hollywood. She fills all of the space on the card that she can.

Also in the mail is her hometown paper which Vee reads cover to cover. It is two weeks old, but there is the article about Gene having been missing and found again. She clips the article for her scrapbook.

A second letter comes from Europe, this one from Jeanie's brother Wayne. Unlike Gene's letters, Wayne has written something the censors thought worthy of blacking out. She tries her best to decipher what is missing, but soon gives up.

At last, Bob's marching orders come. Instead of California, he will be heading to Yuma, Arizona for two months. After that, it could be back to Gowen or on to somewhere else.

"Maybe you should stay here and go back to work at the plant," he suggests. Slightly deflated, he adds, "Or you could go back home."

Vee makes the decision to stay. The girls at the plant welcome her back with smiles and hugs. Unfortunately, Lois has been fired for drinking on the job.

"I warned her," Angie says, "when I smelled liquor on her breath. But then she brought her bottle to work!" In the time Vee has been away, Angie has lightened up considerably. She no longer scolds the line girls for getting a little rowdy, and often joins in their antics.

One Tuesday night, two of the girls decide to marry over break using a ring made from a potato. Angie sanctions the wedding, but the girls are divorced before the shift ends.

With her return to work, Vee feels the pull of something that can all too easily overwhelm her—an independent life. She loves making her own way but fears that, with Bob gone, she may fall too easily for the freedom it represents. After agonizing for several days, she decides to move back to Missouri, back to a place that will ground her. Once more, she gives notice at work, and then begins to pack the things she can send home by parcel post.

# HOME FRONT

# FOURTEEN

**R**uth's husband ships out right after Bob, so Ruth offers to drive Vee as far as Denver and drop her at the bus station. Ruth will head on to Yuma for a few days, and then back to her own parents' home.

They leave around eight in the morning, hoping to make it to Soda Springs for the night. As they drive, the women chat, sing songs and marvel at the beautiful scenery.

"Look at those waterfalls, just coming straight out of the mountainside!"

"And honest-to-goodness covered wagons! I thought Idaho was civilized."

"We'll never get far today if we keep having to stop for all these sheep."

In the closeness of the car, they learn a great deal about each other. Ruth speaks English, Spanish, Japanese, German, Latin, French, and a smattering of other languages. Her step-father is an artist. Vee's father headlines a bluegrass band, and she had won singing contests when she was younger.

Wyoming produces even more road-worthy sheep, slowing their trip to a snail's pace on several occasions. They stop at Little America to refuel before making it in to Denver by 7:00 that evening. The bus to Kansas City has just departed, so Vee buys a ticket for the next departure and fills the time by watching Ginger Rogers in *Lady in the Dark* at a nearby theater.

The 11:00 P.M. bus is nearly empty. She finds a seat near the front and pulls out the last two letters forwarded to her from Gene.

*Somewhere in Italy*
*May 2, 1944*
*Dear Folks,*

*I went to church Sunday. We have a swell chaplain.*

*I'm sending you 200 bucks through the finance department. I'm rolling in money or something. I have very little use for money here.*

*Dad, are you lowering the debt on the 25 acres? Remember, now is the time. My guess is that we will have a very rough depression after this war—so rough that if the 25 isn't yours after the war, you just as well kiss it goodbye. Put part of the money I send you in bonds and part of it in clearing the debt. We should be clear by 1945. I can send at least a hundred every month, usually more.*

*Mom, I should have sent you a souvenir. I will one of these days.*

*I was prowling around in some catacombs below a church somewhere in Italy today. There was an altar built from human bones—beautiful architecture, I guess. There was an old pipe organ.*

*Oh, yes, our plane accident. We landed in water (the Atlantic). The plane sank in a matter of seconds. We all got out – lucky stiffs. We were on a rubber raft about two days. I was in the hospital about a week. I had a lot of cuts and bruises. One bruise on my right hip was rather rough—about a foot long and seven inches wide. I had a cut above my left knee that left a scar about five inches long. I had no broken bones. And, oh yes, I sprained my right ankle. I'm perfectly all right now.*

*Love,*

*Gene*

*May 8, 1944*

*Dear Folks,*

*Mom, I'll answer all your questions about our ditching I can. I censor my own mail, and I'm a rough censor. We hoped the War Department wouldn't be sending telegrams.*

*I can't tell you how far we were from South America when we ditched. We had engine trouble—fire to be exact. We had one of the most successful ditchings ever accomplished. But a rubber raft out in the Atlantic is a lonesome place. A navy destroyer escort (baby destroyer) picked us up. I am in the same plane type as back in the States. Our plane was named "FABO." It was derived from one of the bombardier's famous expressions.*

*We have movies three times a week on the post. We have an old wine cellar as a theater.*

*Your airmail letter came three days ago – the V-mail hasn't even arrived yet. I've only received about five of your letters. Mail service is sometimes very slow. I'm sticking to airmail from now on. I bought 80 envelopes the other day. Airmail moves the fastest.*

*Love,*

*Gene*

*P.S.: If Carmen says "yes" to a certain question I asked her, I'll be married when I next get to the States.*

All the way to Kansas City, Vee imagines her brother and Carmen together, raising a family blended from German and Spanish roots. Her own German heritage came through Tennessee and on to Missouri after many generations. Carmen, on the other hand, is a first-generation citizen from either Spanish or Cuban or Mexican decent. She vows to start writing regularly, hoping to find out more about Carmen's life and family. No matter what her heritage, a sister by law is something to celebrate.

Jeanie fails to meet her at the station in Kansas City at midnight, and Vee cannot find a bus to Martin City. Instead, she falls asleep on a divan in the Ladies Lounge until the morning. A streetcar and bus ride later, she sits in the Long's kitchen and catches up on the family news. Wayne has written from England, though there is little information not edited by the censors. Vee relays all the news about Gene, including his pending engagement.

"Your dad has a new car," Jeanie says the next morning. "But it's too muddy for him to get to town, so Aunt Doris is coming after you."

"He probably just doesn't want to get it dirty."

"Oh, and be prepared," Jeanie warns. "Doris got new false teeth, and she's taking them out and making everyone admire the gums!"

So much has happened to Vee in the previous three months that, when she does make it home, it seems she has been gone for more than a year. Her mom takes her visiting, dragging her from friend to friend so they can talk the latest gossip. She meets up with her brothers Harold Dean and Bob who goes by his last name *Hedrick* as there are far too many Roberts in the world. Vee opens a bank account with the ninety dollars she has brought from Idaho. Later that evening, they visit her in-laws who give Vee her husband's latest allotment check and two letters written home from Yuma, Arizona. It sounds as if he is destined for California after all. She writes to him about her travels home and makes a last-minute diary entry. Before she goes to bed, she rereads a letter from cousin Sophia Barbara whose family moved to California to further her acting career.

*Los Angeles*
*May 3, 1944*
*Dear Velma,*

*That was some letter you wrote and we all enjoyed it. Your other letter was signed "Hammontree" but guess that's a little out of date now, huh? This is a little late to wish you happiness, but we all do. With the wedding news coming in a round about way, it was hard to realize you had really taken the big step. The wedding must have been lovely, and you are very fortunate to have so many nice people near you—and so many your own age, too!*

*We were glad when news of Eugene reached us.*

*Mary is pestering me again. This time she wants to talk about men. I'm in no mood to discuss same—as Bill and I have broken up, for good this time. She says I should have married the brother of a girlfriend I knew in K.C. whose last name was "Pigg." She said she could say "Mrs. Pigg, I'd like you to meet Mr. Charley Horse." We think your friend*

*Corn could be a foot doctor, but of course that's not very original.*

*That was interesting about the Japanese girl, and it is such a shame. They will have a very difficult time of it after the war when and if they return to this state. I wonder how many years it will take to make people tolerant, even of our own Japanese-American veterans.*

*I told Mary what a lousy reputation she's getting as a correspondent. Maybe it will bring results.*

*Love,*

*Sophia Barbara*

*** 

For the next week, Vee relaxes at home, reading, playing with the dog Wiggles or, occasionally, helping her mother with the laundry she takes in to make extra money. There are household chores, like tending to the duck hatchlings that have grown by the minute and are now spilling over the side of the box they are penned up in. On the days she stays home alone, Vee plays the organ or plays "at" her father's fiddle.

"I tried to master the violin, but failed again," she writes half-jokingly to Betty in a letter. "Wouldn't it be wonderful to play in an orchestra?" When her dad catches her listening to classical music on the radio, he scolds her for wasting time on "that uppity music." But she persists. Mozart, Beethoven, Brahms have stolen a piece of her soul, and only by filling her heart with the glorious sounds of *The Magic Flute* or *Moonlight Sonata* can she get it back.

Always, there are the countless letters to and from Bob, Jeanie, Wayne, Betty, Gene, and now Carmen del Llano.

*Somewhere in Italy*

*May 15, 1944*

*Dear Folks,*

*Mom, I didn't get to write to you yesterday (Mother's Day). I was too busy to even have time to think. I do want to say this—you're a swell mother. You couldn't be beat. The same goes for Dad and the rest of the family. I wish I could be home for Thanksgiving this year.*

*So you think you would like Carmen for a daughter-in-law? I know you would. Such will be the case if she says "yes." I think she will. I'll be getting an answer soon. She is definitely the one for me. She is very sweet. The first place I go when I get back to the States is Tampa or wherever else Carmen is. The next place is Harrisonville, of course. Didn't I go a long way to find the girl I was looking for?*

*These clumsy bombardiers—our light cord has been accidentally pulled out twice and both times by bombardiers, my bombardier included. I was proud of him the day before yesterday. I'll tell you about it sometime. It can't be written. He did just what I would have done had I been in his place. He's a good man for a bombardier.*

*This is much better than the roar of engines, the swish of airflow around an airplane fuselage, and "the flak" (antiaircraft fire, German).*

*I better stop and grab a snack. I had no breakfast—I slept too late—I was plenty tired.*

*Love,*

*Gene*

May 17, 1944

Dear Folks,

*I had plenty of sleep last night with no flying to worry about today. We've had several buzz jobs this morning. One plane almost knocked a tent down.*

*About half the food I eat is K rations, and they're not bad, usually better than what our cooks cook up. On missions, we always eat K rations.*

*There never is any news, and when there is, it's too hot to handle. Like ditching—we couldn't mention it but the War Department did and how. I thought that it had been broadcast on a national radio hookup. Doesn't bad news travel fast?*

*I got your letter yesterday. A different car, eh?*

*I hope Claude Ament has better luck getting over than I did. Wouldn't it be funny if I would run into him over here? If I do, it won't be unusual. I've seen a lot of fellows here I haven't seen for a long time.*

*We have a pretty good tent. When it rains, it's nice to lay in the sack and hear the rain gently tapping the tent.*

*Ending my note with love,*

*Gene*

Carmen sends a lovely Mother's Day card to Vee's mom. If Mildred had any reservations about Carmen's suitability as a daughter-in-law, they melt away. Vee, of course, has already decided to like Gene's girl, and the two of them begin a weekly correspondence. Vee loves opening the envelope to Carmen's flowing script.

*Tampa, Florida*
*May 20, 1944*
*Dear Vee,*

*Just got home from a plane crash. Just two blocks from home, it was really terrible. I'll send you the article and picture of it. I cried because I saw the boys suffering, and I thought how much more Gene suffered.*

*You certainly have traveled since you got married. I wish you all the luck in the world, and may God keep you two in the best of health always. Are you going to go with your husband again? You are very lucky to have him here in the states with you, as many boys are going over as soon as they complete their three-month training.*

*We haven't heard from brother yet, and we're all very worried about him. We might get a letter from him Monday.*

*I'm going to send you some more of that piano music you like to play. We can get some down here for a very low price, so don't be surprised if you receive some, some day. Does Gene play the piano? We have a piano at home, but I can't play. I took lessons for one year, but had to quit them.*

*We had a Mother's Day banquet, and I was the soloist. I sang several songs. I was awfully nervous, but later got over it as they were all very nice and understood why I was shaking. I sang "our favorite" Stardust and had to repeat it for them.*

*Please tell Mother Hammontree that I'm having some pictures made, and just as soon as I get them, I will send her one, and you also. I have one of you as Gene left it home one night. It's a very nice picture of you.*

*Sending all my love and luck to an unseen friend whom I long to see very much. I remain*
*Always,*
*Carmen*
*P.S. Will have more to write in my next letter as now I'm still a little upset about the plane crash.*

# HOME FRONT

# FIFTEEN

*Somewhere in Italy*
*May 26, 1944*
*Dear Folks,*

*There's a story behind the reason I didn't have my big deal hat in those pictures. I had those taken after I met Carmen. The first night I was with her, we went riding on those electric automobiles at one of Tampa's carnivals. Anyway, my big deal hat fell under a car and received rough treatment. Enough said.*

*Mom, I'll get you a souvenir yet. I heard about a certain store in a certain town somewhere in Italy where there would be a good possibility for a good souvenir.*

*Some articles cost very much here compared to there. Italians think we're millionaires. A radio worth $20 costs $250. Eggs are 15 cents apiece.*

*Velma, so you and Bob like Stardust, too. What do you know.*

*In about an hour, we go to chow. Then we have a meeting with the colonel—about what, we don't know. It could be almost anything.*

*Love,*
*Gene*

Toward the end of May, Vee becomes restless. When Jeanie and Wayne's brother Clifton visit one evening, he talks about his new job at Pratt & Whitney in Kansas City.

"With this war dragging on, they really need workers. They're hiring just about anybody that can get through the training."

Vee seriously thinks it over. She misses working—the camaraderie and the paycheck. Building airplane engines should be infinitely more interesting than specking potatoes. The only problem is finding a place to live.

Jeanie has the answer. "Come stay with us until you get something lined up!" Her parents' home in Martin City has quick bus access to the Kansas City metro area. Once there, a streetcar can take them almost anywhere in the city they care to go.

It is the push Vee needs. She packs her suitcase and heads out again. This time, she will be more intentional about work. And about play. She has the whole of Kansas City to roam with her best friend, Jeanie.

"This darn war," Mrs. Long complains one day. "Not a new needle to be had anywhere! I'd buy a new machine just to get the needle if they didn't have them on rations, too." She looks at her daughter. "By the way, Jeanie, where did you put my last sugar stamp?"

Jeanie shrugs. "It was on the kitchen counter last I saw it."

"Well, you'd best look for it, or I can't bake any pies this week. I'm down to my last cup."

The next morning, Vee and Jeanie take the bus downtown. They walk to Jeanie's brother's apartment as a jumping-off point while job searching. Ken, his wife Loretta, and their twins live in a converted second-floor apartment in a large two-story home on Brooklyn Avenue. Since Jeanie is still too young for the factory job, she applies and is instantly hired at the nearby Sears department store.

"Well, I've decided not to work at Sears," Jeanie informs Vee the next day. "I'm going to try for P&W, too."

"But you're not old enough."

"So. If you go with me to the library and pretend to be my sister, we can say I lost my birth certificate."

Their subterfuge is unsuccessful.

At Katz, they stop for a hamburger, but with meat in scarce supply, they settle for butterscotch sundaes with whipped cream.

"Funny the things you can eat when you have no choice," Vee says. "What I would have given for a sundae back in the Depression."

Vee makes her first attempt to interview at Pratt & Whitney, but is informed that she will need a release from the War Manpower Commission. She makes a trip to the commission offices the next day, but comes away without the necessary paperwork for P&W, though they do refer her to the Brunson Instrument Company. A second trip to the commission produces a second letter of recommendation for, "...of all things, the Battenfeld Grease and Oil Company!" Even with the extensive bus and trolley system, Battenfeld is devilishly hard to get to, although it does pay 61 cents an hour to start, and time and a half overtime on all Saturdays.

Both of the girls are hired on at Battenfeld. They decide to stay in Ken and Loretta's spare bedroom, and still they are up at 5:30 to get to work on time.

"It takes hours to get to that dump on the streetcar," Vee complains to Loretta the first evening. "But a lady who calls herself Joe found us a ride with Jack *somebody*."

Loretta combs her twin girls' hair and nods absently as Vee rambles on.

"The work is okay. I work with Minnie. Jeanie works with Lorena. She is really nice. Martha is so-so. She'll do. There is a guy who reminds me of Frankie Wright. I dislike him with all my soul."

After dinner, Loretta and the twins, Mary Kay and Betty Faye, take turns playing the piano while Vee reads through the mail that Ken brings in.

"Say, Vee," Mary Kay asks after finishing a duet. "How old does a person have to be before they can get married?"

"Why? Are you thinking about it?"

Betty Faye giggles and pushes her sister's shoulder. "She's got a boyfriend. But he doesn't know it yet."

"Oh, the woes of the younger generation," Vee says, feigning concern. "I think you should wait a year or two since you're only eight." She looks back at her letters. "Miss Elizabeth Louise Corn says that some of the girls got fired at *The Company* today. The lucky kids! I almost never want to eat a potato again. Almost."

Ken rattles his newspaper and says, "We got a new drink machine at the plant today. It's built like a juke box, but with three kinds of drinks. You put in a nickle and push a button for the drink you want."

"Amazing," Loretta says as she clears the table. "Instead of a juke box, it's a juice box."

Jack picks the girls up on workdays at 7:30. One morning at the plant, a jar of some unknown chemical brakes and sends the workers running from the smell. Fire trucks come to help with cleanup while Vee and Jeanie are shuffled to another department for the rest of the day.

"It was the worst department in the place!" Vee complains. "I hope we don't have to do that again tomorrow."

On the weekend, the extended family packs their swim suits and summer gear for a trip to Swope Park with the elder Longs. The June sunshine warms the bustling park as what seems like the entire population of Kansas City flocks to the open spaces. While the men fish, the girls walk miles to find bikes to rent, but there are none available, so they settle for a hasty tour of the zoo.

"This is the life," Vee says. "There's so much to do in the city!"

On Tuesday June 6th, their supervisor at Battenfeld's seeks out Jeanie and Vee. "I have to apologize to you ladies," Mr. Babbit says. "I didn't think you'd stay this long."

Jeanie rolls her eyes. "Well, as long as you don't put us in the *hole* again!"

"Yeah, that was filthy work. Not fit for *proper* ladies." Vee cannot decide which is more demeaning—slopping grease, specking potatoes, or slapping 352 labels on quarts of Shingle Stick in one day.

Over lunch break, the cafeteria is abuzz with gossip. "D Day," someone says. "The invasion begins!" Jeanie and Vee stare gravely at their meals. Gene and Wayne are probably in the thick of it.

"I hope they'll always be safe," Vee says, almost in prayer. "And as many of the other boys as possible."

Minnie nods toward the men in the room. "I imagine these boys still in the States wish they could be in the thick of it."

For the rest of the afternoon, the workers go diligently but silently about their work as a radio gives chilling news about what is happening in Europe. It seems everyone in the building has a family member or friend involved in the fighting on some front. Most have no true idea where their loved-ones are stationed, so the push on the beaches of Normandy touches a personal nerve for all.

And then someone accidentally spills a Coke on the radio, shorting it out. A collective "NOOOOO!" rises up from the factory floor.

Jack has plans for the evening. Instead of riding the dawdling trolley home, the girls decide to walk the ten city blocks from the bottoms, up the steep slopes toward downtown Kansas City and back to Brooklyn Avenue.

"Oh, my aching feet!" Vee complains as she tosses her shoes on the floor. "I don't know how much more of this I can take."

Loretta and the girls set the table for dinner. "I don't suppose I have to ask how work went, then."

"Work was horrid. Lunch was fun, though. That Rom sure kills us with his jokes. Says he has a job up in the office doing draft work. He opens and shuts the windows." They all laugh.

Her face sobers. "I think I want to go home this weekend. Maybe they've heard something from Gene."

Loretta nods understanding. She, too, is worried about both Wayne and Dude. "We'll drive you to the folks' on Friday and you can catch the bus from Martin City."

# HOME FRONT

# SIXTEEN

**The weekend proves a good distraction.** Vee's Grandmother Kohntopp has received a wedding invitation from Hollywood. Ella's great-nephew Gail Shikles Jr.—better known in the world as the handsome film and television star Craig Stevens—is marrying the Canadian-born actress Alexis Smith. Their wedding is the talk of Harrisonville and gives Ella minor celebrity status for a while.

There are letters from Betty and Mrs. Corn, and one to her mom from Carmen. The Long's receive a letter from Wayne, but it is dated before June 6th and does little to resolved their worries.

The entire family attends Sunday school and church the next morning. The nave at the Pleasant Ridge Baptist Church is filled to overflowing with regular members and with others who attend only sporadically. News on the world stage seems to draw them all together on this particular Sunday.

When time comes to head back to the city, Vee hates to leave. Her mother looks forlorn. All of them worry about Gene, and even though

Mildred had not given birth to them, Vee, Gene, and Harold Dean could not feel more loved. Mildred built a strong bond—effortlessly it seems—between the two blended families. To Vee, Mildred is *Mom*.

Work, on the other hand, stresses Vee to the limits. Not only is it physically demanding, but personalities begin to clash. By the end of the week, she makes a cryptic diary entry. "Waked. Arose. Ate. Waited. Dressed. Woiked. Cussed. Ate. Loafed. Woiked. Cussed. Sang. Laughed. Whistled. Loafed. Woiked. Rode. Looked. Arrived. Left. Walked. Shopped. Bought. Returned. Ate. Sang. Wrote. I get so mad at Flo, I could give her the hot foot!"

And so ends her brief run at Battenfeld Grease and Oil. Belongings in hand, Vee rides the bus to Harrisonville once more.

> *June 10 1944*
> *Dear Folks,*
>
> > *I'm somewhere in Russia—taking life relatively easy most of the time. This is just a note to let you know I'm all right.*
> > *Love,*
> > *Gene*

Everyone breathes a sigh of relief that Gene is so prompt in writing. Bob has not written for several days, but Vee knows he is still safe stateside. Perhaps they are moving him again. Too many families have not heard from their sons and husbands, and with the Allied push, so many of them will now be in harm's way.

> *Somewhere in Italy*
> *June 11, 1944*
> *Dear Folks,*
>
> > *We don't definitely have our own plane yet. I don't know what we'll call it. One suggestion was "Sea Puppy" but that reminds us too much of the fact that "FABO" is down in Davy Jones' locker.*
> > *Carmen sent me the cutest snapshot of herself in a bathing suit and does she look good! But she looks good in anything—take it from me. And is she sweet, ah. She is the*

*swellest girl in every way I've ever had the pleasure to know.*

*Carmen's folks were really nice to me. Half of my dates with Carmen were right at her home. Their house is spotless and neat. Yes, Carmen is Catholic.*

*I haven't received her answer, yet, but here's hoping. I bet you thought I would never talk like this about any girl for quite a while, but I have found the girl I was looking for. The first time I met her, I liked her. The third time, I started falling for her in a big way and didn't know it then. As soon as I left her, I was certain. There's no use to argue with love. So here I am wanting to say "I do" with her.*

*I sent you a note while I was stationed in Russia. Because of strict censorship, it may never reach you. The Russians were really friendly. From what I saw, I can see why they can drive back the Germans. While we were there, some Russian players put on a series of opera sketches and dances, Russian style. I wouldn't have missed it.*

*I better sign off*
*With love,*
*Gene*

*June 18, 1944*
*Dear Folks,*

*The country is much like the States. The climate now is like that of Missouri except the nights are cooler.*

*I am going to rest camp very soon. The rest of the officers in my crew are going, too. We'll get away from flak for awhile, anyway.*

*Love,*
*Gene*

*Tampa, Florida*
*June 19, 1944*
*Dear Vee,*

*Please forgive me for not answering your letter sooner, but I have been very busy. I like classical music, also. I bought "Tonight We Love" from the movie Song of Russia. Have you seen it? If not, don't miss it.*

*Sunday noon we went to a wedding. It was a beautiful ceremony. I don't know why, but every time I go to a wedding, I cry. She was one of my girlfriends. When Gene was*

*here, she bet that we would get married before she would, but it was all the opposite. She
didn't get to wear a wedding gown, because he came from overseas sooner than he expected.
Oh, it really was a very beautiful ceremony.*

*My brother wrote last week and told us why he delayed to write. He's still in New
Guinea and was out in the jungles for two months. I hope he comes home soon as it's been
almost three years that we haven't seen him.*

*Please send me a photo of you and your husband, and in return, I will send you
one of myself.*

*I'll close sending all my love to you.*

*Always,*

*Carmen*

Vee still has her eyes set on Pratt & Whitney, so she turns down an offer
to work at the local grocery store. Not only will the factory job be better
pay, but it seems more important than ever to support the boys overseas in
their efforts to stamp out tyranny. She helps her mother and father through
the week, and on the weekends, she spends the night at her in-laws. One
Friday night, Mildred shows up with Bob in tow.

"Why didn't you write?" everyone asks. "Why didn't you tell us you
were coming?"

Bob shrugs it off. "The army. They never tell us anything until the last
minute." His eyes give off a twinkle of mischief knowing he has surprised
them all. He stands tall and proud in his uniform.

They make the rounds to see family and friends—Bob sharing what he
knows about anyone connected to home. After Sunday-morning services,
it seems the entire countryside has gathered for a picnic. They talk all
evening and into the night, lounging under the old elm tree behind the
Pleasant Ridge church.

"They're finally shipping me to California," Bob tells Vee late in the
evening. "Come with me."

"Let me think about it," she says, unsure yet if it would be the right
decision. "How long are you going to be here?"

"Furlough is a week."

They treat themselves to as much fun as they can over the next few days—shopping in the city and visiting Swope and Fairyland Parks. In late evening, they lay on blankets in the yard to watch the moon rise or *park* at the old cemetery—something Vee thinks husbands and wives should do more often.

Gene and Carmen continue to write, and everyone waits on pins and needles to know what Carmen will say to his proposal.

*Somewhere in Italy*
*June 27, 1944*
*Dear Sis,*

*How's tricks? Good, no doubt.*

*I get back from Russia, then what do they do to me—they hustle me off to rest camp. I got back from rest camp yesterday. Rest? H'm. I'm pooped. I rode horses, fished, took boat rides, rode bicycles, and even took a stab at tennis. A mental rest is the purpose of a rest camp, so I guess the purpose was accomplished.*

*Only one thing now—I need a rest from rest camp. It was pretty up in the mountains away from civilization, up in the pines. What a place that would be for a honeymoon!*

*Yes, I have been on missions—quite. That's one reason I have been to camp. You'll have to guess the type plane I'm flying. We named it "FLAT 50." I can't tell you why.*

*I'm a rough censor, but I'm playing safe. I don't want to ever get caught with my letters down. I better stop for now.*

*Love,*
*Gene*

*Tampa, Florida*
*June 28, 1944*
*Dear Pruneface,*

*I certainly adore that name. They call you crazy names it's true, but they're awfully cute. I can hardly wait to see all of you in person (oh lucky day).*

*Maybe we could have an orchestra someday, with all those instruments and my singing, right? I can play the clarinet. I'd love to hear the banjo. You'll have to play it for me someday.*

*You follow your husband as long as you possibly can, as after he goes over, you wouldn't see him for a long time. Show him a good time as long as you can.*

*I just got a letter from Gene today. None from Brother. Gene never tells me much about himself. I sent him two packages already, and he doesn't mention anything in the letters. Maybe he hasn't received them yet.*

*I'm going to go to work at a drug store as an assistant pharmacist. I may not even like that type of work, but there's no harm in trying.*

*Until tomorrow. May God watch over you.*

*Love and kisses,*

*Carmen*

*Somewhere in Italy*

*June 30, 1944*

*Dear Folks,*

*Mom I'm sending you some Italian currency. There was a nice handmade bedspread in a store somewhere in Italy that I had my eye on. Somebody beat me to it. It is very hard to find anything typical of Italy.*

*You know, a mosquito net is all right, keeping away mosquitoes by night and flies by day. A fellow can sleep with flies all over the place when he's under a net. I can sleep best right after a mission.*

*Love,*

*Gene*

# SEVENTEEN

**F**urlough is coming to an end, and Vee feels pressured to travel to California with her husband. Having a better idea of what her needs will be, she packs three suitcases for the trip. On their last day in Missouri, they spend the morning and afternoon with immediate family at an outing in Swope Park—touring the zoo, swimming, and boating in the scalding sun. In late evening, the family drives them to Union Station to catch the train.

The couple settles into a Portland car. They are not able to lay down to sleep on bench seats as Vee had done on her previous train trip, but at least they can lean on each other. The conductor wakes them at 7:00 in the morning to punch their tickets.

Every other town, it seems, demands a layover. Vee makes note of the number of times they change trains, of the gas lights and the signs stating "Do not shoot buffalo from platform." At one point, she looks out at what appears to be an ocean—the Great Salt Lake. It stretches for fifty miles before drying into salt plains and then sand hills. In contrast, the country from Reno to the California line is the prettiest she has ever seen.

From Sacramento to Lemoore, where Bob is stationed, Vee is sure they would have made better time on a handcar. They leave the train just outside the air field. When they inquire about a bus ticket to Hanford, the ticket agent tells them it would be quicker and easier to hitchhike the eight miles. An accommodating driver drops them at the Hanford USO, where a Mr. Curtis calls and calls to find someone willing to take them in for the night. At last one of the locals is happy to do her part for a soldier in uniform, and Vee is ecstatic to have a bath after four days traveling.

With two days left on his furlough, Bob helps Vee settle into Mrs. Warnock's rooming house. They explore the community, deciding on their favorite restaurant—Harry's. At the USO, they play pool and fight over which songs to play on the juke box. Soon, it is time for Bob to grab his barracks bag and hitch a ride back to Lemoore.

Once again, Vee is on her own. She writes to family, Carmen, and Betty Corn to give them the boardinghouse address. Braver now, she spends afternoons wandering Hanford's Chinatown to shop and try their cultural cuisine. Girls at the boardinghouse—Ola and Charlene (or Charley, as she likes to be called)—offer their friendship. Ola is engaged to be married that very night to a lieutenant named Don, though Charley says she does not love her intended. The two women help another girl, Cherry, catch a ride for the bus station after deciding to leave her new husband. In all of the turmoil around the wartime relationships, Charley and Dempsey's seems to be the most secure. Vee wishes she loved Bob that much.

Within the week, her first packet of forwarded letters arrive.

*Tampa, Florida*
*July 4, 1944*
*Dear Vee,*

*What a grand celebration we had today—a parade early in the morning and then later in the day, a rodeo. We had a large group singing patriotic songs. Our mayor gave a wonderful speech on the subject of the fighting men who are now giving their lives for us.*

*I heard from Gene last week. He tells me more details of his crash, poor thing. He went through a lot, and says he's got a few scars and bad memories.*

*Good for me, I got hold of a package of chewing gum. Boy is it hard to get any down here. The only way we can get it is by ordering some three weeks ahead, and then we may not even get any after all. Gene used to bring me a package every week, but since he's gone, so is the gum.*

*I'll have to call this quits. It's already passed my bedtime.*

*All my love,*

*Carmen*

*Somewhere in Italy*

*July 4, 1944*

*Dear Sis,*

*Brother's all right. Still kickin'.*

*I'm sorry, Vee, but our plane is already named—"FLAT 50." Though you suggested some good ones.*

*Thank you for the birthday card. I had forgotten I had one. H'm. I'm getting flak-happy again and only back from rest camp about two weeks ago.*

*Talking about people—I admire the Russians more than any other people over here. One thing I regret is not knowing all foreign languages. Of course, I learn some words of each. The Russian language is probably one of the hardest to learn to write (my opinion). Greek is rough, too—maybe much rougher.*

*Joe, my bombardier, was just discussing his days as first sergeant in an observation squadron. He was rough as he still pretends to be—you know, the old first sergeant attitude. He and I are plenty goofy. Joe is as wild a jeep driver as I am. Two fellows rode a few miles with him today and then they wanted out. They were afraid he was going to ground-loop. Jeeps really handle nice.*

*With the aid of a large hammer, a pair of pliers, and a trench knife, Joe took the error out of his wristwatch the other day. Fact is, he took everything out. He mentioned something about the mainspring not being straight. Need I say, Joe now has no timepiece?*

*Carmen isn't very temperamental. She's so darned sweet, it hurts. When she is teasing somebody, she has the cutest twinkle in her eyes.*

*I better sign off*

*With love,*

*Gene*

*July 6, 1944*

*Dear Folks,*

*So that letter had a mushy note? H'm. And why not? I don't fall in love every day. It was about time I found "the one." It's a darned shame it had to be just before I left the USA.*

*I guess I am a wild jeep driver. I remember one time I went between two wagons (two-wheeled Italian wagons) missing one on the left side by three inches and the one on the right side by two inches. I don't think I'll do that again. I stick my neck out enough without trying to ground-loop a jeep.*

*Oxen are used some here. More oxen are used in southern Italy than farther north. So long for now.*

*Love,*

*Gene*

Better acquainted with her boardinghouse mates, Vee lunches frequently at Pedon's where both Ola and Charley work. In their off hours, Vee and the girls hike in the woods or go to the beautiful Fox theater with its private balcony "boxes" and blinking star ceiling.

When she is on her own, she buys fresh fruit from the Chinese food market, or listens to Mrs. Warnock's phonograph, or goes to the library to read whatever poetry she finds. When she is truly bored, she tries her hand at writing verse.

"Nonsense," she gripes after scribbling a few lines. "I'll never make the grade. Wish I could write one killer poem just once, then I could die and say I'd done something."

With so much free time, she pens dozens of letters each week, sometimes finding little to actually fill the pages. The news is as boring as her routine until one Sunday morning when a nearby Negro camp meeting wakes her from a deep sleep. She lays in bed and listens to the crooning. For an hour, the organ moans, and men and women take turns soloing the verse, and all sing the chorus. Vee does not believe she has ever heard anything quite so beautiful.

"Bob doesn't know how right he was when he said I went to church just to hear the music," she whispers to her pillow. "It takes me nearer to heaven than anything anyone could say."

Still, the music, her time with the girls, and her limited amount of time with Bob are not enough to ease her restlessness. With so many women living near the base, wanting to be near their husbands or boyfriends, work is scarce. But it is more than that for Vee. She realizes that her heart has become restless for something outside of her marriage—someone that she has more in common with. Secretly, she begins to envy Cherry.

On July 18th—a fateful day for more reasons than she can imagine—Vee buys a train ticket for home.

# HOME FRONT

# EIGHTEEN

**H**aving lost her mother before the age of four, Vee had unconsciously built an emotional wall around her feelings. Growing up with two brothers and two step-brothers did not do much to open her up. She is close to her step-mom, Mildred, yet she reveals her deepest feelings to no one. Not even to Jeanie.

Carmen is the first genuine confidant in her life. A true sister-to-be, Vee feels the two of them coming closer together with each exchange of letters. Carmen's sweet nature shines through her carefully-scripted words and the kind and caring deeds she writes about. And there is something about the distance, the anonymity of this women she has never met. Vee trusts her. So much so that she writes of her desire to divorce Bob. She posts the letter before boarding the train.

On the platform in Barstow, a young soldier named Al helps Vee on board with her suitcases and then takes a seat beside her. When the train is underway, Al and two of his buddies involve Vee in a friendly game of casino.

"You're letting me win," she accuses Al after the fourth game.

"Maybe," he says with a shrug. "But we've got a long trip ahead of us. Anything could happen."

Al is headed to Chicago, while "Sarge" and Chuck are going on to Detroit. The four of them share a bit about their backgrounds, and before they reach the California state line, the boys are fawning over Vee, telling her what a swell dame she is. She enjoys the attention, particularly from Al.

"With a guy like that," she thinks to herself, "I could get a long way in this world."

The four of them hop off the train at El Navajo to look over the silver and turquoise jewelry offered by the locals. They buy oranges and potato chips, but the boys will not eat the oranges until Vee has peeled them. She enjoys their flattering attention, the laughter, and especially her deep discussions with Mr. Dildarian.

"I make my sister play *Prelude in C# Minor* all the time," Al says as he finishes a sandwich from the lunch car.

"Oh, I love Rachmaninoff! But especially Mozart. He's my absolute favorite." The more she learns about him, the more handsome Al looks in her eyes—his dark wavy hair, beautiful brown eyes, his quiet old-fashioned manner. But it is what they have in common that draws her to him. He loves classical music, books and crossword puzzles. He lives in New York— something that appeals to Vee more since her experience living in a large city, if only for a couple of weeks.

The train stops in Albuquerque for a long layover, so the four compatriots go in search of a nice restaurant.

"Nothing but beer joints," Vee says, pouting. "I don't like beer."

Al grabs her hand and pulls her toward a fruit stand. "What would you like? Grapes? Peaches? Plums?" He sacks up her choices and picks out a cake.

Back on the train, they share the fruit, and then Chuck pulls his airman's wings off his uniform and uses them to cut the cake into several pieces. "Why not?" he asks with a shrug. "I've used them to cut cheese before."

That night, Vee sleeps the best she has ever slept on a train. She opens her eyes in time to see the most beautiful sunrise over the Colorado plains. It fills her heart with joy until she realizes that her time with Al will soon come to an end. She wishes she had the courage to ask for his address, to stay connected, but she still has so much of her own life to sort out.

At Union Station, Al and Chuck help carry her suitcases to the street car stop. They bid her goodbye, and she makes her way to Brooklyn Avenue, and Ken and Loretta's apartment.

***

Vee tries again for a position at Pratt & Whitney. The first time back, she is turned away, but her persistence pays off a few days later. She will need a physical and training. The exam by the company doctors reveals a low heart-rate and bad tonsils, but they clear her for any work that is required. She starts classes the very next evening.

Night classes are interesting even though they cut into her social life and time spent with her best friend. When they can, she and Jeanie roam the city together—shopping, eating, watching movies, enjoying activities at Swope Park and PlaMor. On occasion, she joins Jeanie and a beau or two for nights on the town. She thinks of herself as a chaperon—a fourth wheel—and not a married woman cheating on her husband. She convinces herself that it does not matter as long as she does not sleep with anyone. One thing is certain. She is falling in love with city life.

She makes friends with her classmates. Pat O'Hara—who used to tap dance with a road show—is really named Juanita Millner. She recently bought an $18 present for a boyfriend who "quit" her, so she returned the gift and bought a cute slacks suit to catch another man.

There is Miss Troutman, and Mrs. Farris who rhymes with Mr. Paris who is cute. Kit and Wilma come to class with hangovers. Ritchie from Mobile is double-jointed. Hudson has a couple of weak fingers. Vee spends breaks sitting with Bob's Aunt Opal, who also works there.

Vee tests well on her papers—making a hundred percent in Blueprint, Math and Precision. For ten tests over two days, her average score is ninety-eight percent. She likes the mental challenge, and she likes the atmosphere. More than anything, she loves the independence.

*Tampa, Florida*
*August 4, 1944*
*Dearest Vee,*

*Your letter took some time to get here, but it's better late than never. I wrote to Gene last night. I haven't heard from him for quite a while.*

*I was awfully sorry to hear about you and Bob. I guess if you stay away from him for a while you'll start loving him again. I do hope so. I guess one thing you did wrong was to still have your girl friends. I mean, go out with them as you did while still single. When one gets married, you can still have your friends but not go out as you did. Please, whatever I say, don't get angry at me as it's really my opinion, and whatever you think is right, you should do. Try not to divorce him. Above all, do your best to make him happy. Try again, Vee. You have your whole life before you, so do your best to make it a happy life. If you see that for the second time it doesn't work, do the thing you think will be best.*

*I'm awfully glad to hear about your new job. You'll be making and earning quite a large amount of money.*

*I mailed Gene a package this morning. I do hope I get some mail from him tomorrow. I'm starting to get worried. He's been working so hard. I guess that's why he doesn't write.*

*I must leave now to visit a hospital patient, so this means I'll have to close.*
*All my love,*
*Carmen*

On Sunday, Vee and Jeanie catch the bus to Harrisonville where her parents meet them at the station. She has not seen her father and mother since leaving for California. After a warm hug, her mother hands her a telegram and prefaces it with a cautious frown.

*Washington DC*
*1128 pm 8/4/44*
*Truman Hammontree Harrisonville Mo*
  *The Secretary of War desires me to express his deep regret that your son Second Lieut Eugene L. Hammontree has been reported missing in action since eighteen July over Germany. If further details or other information are received you will be promptly notified.*
  *Ulio,*
  *The Adjutant General*

Vee stares hard at the telegram, willing the words to disappear. She looks again at the date Gene went missing—the same day she bought her ticket to leave California.

"I can't believe anything's happened to him. I'm going to write him," she says, as if that simple act will conjure some magic. "And just when I'm realizing what a wonderful brother he is."

There is hope in the fact that Gene had gone missing before and was recovered alive and relatively well. She begs Jeanie to spend the night with her. After dinner, the girls climb the stairs of her parent's house to the attic bedrooms where Jeanie hugs her friend as she cries herself to sleep one more time.

***

When Vee returns to work, life in the city has temporarily lost its luster. She leans on Loretta for moral support, confessing her wish to divorce Bob. Loretta makes no judgments, but simply gives Vee a safe place to express her emotions and talk through her issues.

Vee's testing scores fall off at work. "At least I'm not fired, yet," she tells Loretta. "They really tried to scare us, though."

Through all of the emotional turmoil, the thing that steadies her the most are the letters from Carmen.

*Tampa, Florida*
*August 11, 1944*
*Dearest Vee,*

    *I am glad to hear that you came home for the weekend with Jeanie. I know how shocked you were to hear of Gene's news. Vee, I haven't slept but thirty minutes these past three nights. I hope nothing has happened to him. I don't know what I'd do.*

    *I had to read Mom's letter three or four times. I thought I was reading things and seeing things. The first thing I read was the newspaper clipping, and I was crying with pride to know he was awarded the medal, but when I read Mom's letter, oh, I can't tell how horrible I felt. Vee, he just has to come back, and I know he will. I know I shouldn't take it so hard because he's only reported missing, and there's a great chance for him to show up. He may be held a prisoner, and he may have been captured by the Underground Forces. I have gone to the Red Cross, and they will try to inform me as soon as they receive any news. I'll write his commanding officer. I know he'll notify me as soon as he knows any information.*

    *Please, if you receive any information, write me and tell me all about it.*

    *Have you heard anything of Bob? I guess he's still in California, right? I do hope you get together again. Please try.*

    *Luck and all my love.*

    *Always,*

    *Carmen*

Carmen's letter echoes Vee's own thoughts—that Gene must be alive somewhere under circumstances that simply do not allow him to communicate. That feeling is reinforced by Major General Ulio in a separate letter.

*The Adjutant General's Office*
*11 August 1944*
*Dear Mr. Hammontree:*

    *This letter is to confirm my recent telegram in which you were regretfully informed that your son, Second Lieutenant Eugene L. Hammontree, has been reported missing in action since 18 July 1944 over Germany.*

*The term "missing in action" is used only to indicate that the whereabouts or status of an individual is not immediately known. It is not intended to convey the impression that the case is closed. I wish to emphasize that every effort is exerted continuously to clear up the status of our personnel. Under war conditions this is a difficult task as you must readily realize. Experience has shown that many persons reported missing in action are subsequently reported as prisoners of war, but as this information is furnished by countries with which we are at war, the War Department is helpless to expedite such reports. However, in order to relieve financial worry, Congress has enacted legislation which continues in force the pay, allowances and allotments to dependents of personnel being carried in a missing status.*

*Permit me to extend to you my heartfelt sympathy during this period of uncertainty.*

*Sincerely yours,*

*J. A. Ulio*

*Adjutant General*

*Tampa, Florida*

*August 15, 1944*

*Dear Vee,*

*Just got through reading this afternoon's paper, and much to my surprise saw an article about a Tampa boy who is also missing over Germany. I called his mother, and she tells me she is sure that he is in the very same plane as Gene's. I'm sending you the clipping.*

*My girlfriend's brother was reported missing since August 4. She received word from the War Department Saturday. It was his first mission. We do hope he shows up. All of them will before this is over.*

*I had my picture taken. As soon as I get them, I'll mail you and Mom one. I bought a beautiful frame for your picture, and oh it really looks sharp. Don't tell anyone, but I talk to it every day. I kiss Gene's picture before going to bed. I haven't missed a single day.*

*Bob is going overseas, isn't he? When you write him, try to be cheerful. Try not to hurt him in any way. They go through quite a lot of hardships when they go over.*

*This last week, I embroidered some guest towels and some pillow cases for my hope chest. I might as well continue with it as I have hope that Gene will return soon. I don't care how long I'll have to wait for him.*

*All my love always,*

*Carmen (Sis)*

# HOME FRONT

# NINETEEN

**Carmen's admonition strikes a chord for Vee, so she continues writing to Bob, keeping her letters positive without committing too much to their future.** She writes about Gene—hopeful. As tenuous as that hope is, it's reinforced by a letter from Gene's squadron commander.

*August 20, 1944*
*Dear Mrs. Hammontree,*

*I am writing this letter to spare you any unnecessary grief and anxiety. I am already in receipt of your letter stating that the War Department notified you your son was missing. I know how brief their messages can be even though it is a question of necessity. At the same time, I like to feel that I may describe the action a little less formally. Eugene is one of my better navigators and a good friend.*

*Our group was assigned to destroy a very important target in Germany. On its way to the target, the group became separated from our fighter escort because of bad weather. Alone and without a moment's hesitation, our group began its bomb run in the face of about 200 enemy fighters. Against such over-whelming odds, there was absolutely no possibility to escape without the loss of some airplanes.*

*When I first counted the returning airplanes, I suffered the same anguish that must have been yours upon receiving the message from Washington—you see, I lost all the airplanes in my squadron. However, when we consolidated the eyewitness accounts, I learned that the sky was filled with parachutes in the immediate vicinity of my squadron. Since then, I've had high hopes of seeing all my men again soon or after this war has ended. I'm sure you will agree, we have every reason to believe that Eugene is alive and well, although he may be a prisoner.*

*In the event I finish my tour of duty overseas before this war is over, I should be very happy to be welcomed into your home. In the meantime, if there is anything I can do to further help you, please feel free to call on me at any time.*

*Sincerely,*

*Fred J. Ascani*

Because Gene has already sent his mother a list of stateside addresses, Mildred, takes the opportunity to write to the mothers and wives of Gene's crew mates—networking so they can share any scrap of news between them. As the days tick by with no word, Mildred grows more anxious and less inclined to write Carmen. She cannot process her son's circumstance without having to consider a future that might not come to pass.

Vee, on the other hand, finds her exchanges with Carmen a true comfort.

*Tampa, Florida*

*August 24, 1944*

*Dearest Vee,*

*I'm awfully worried about Mom. She hasn't written me since I sent her a Special Delivery. Please tell me what's wrong.*

*Thank you very much for that beautiful birthday card. That was a very sweet poem you wrote. I received many gifts—the best was a 36 convertible sedan. It's green and in very good shape. I don't get to go riding very much as there's still this gas rationing.*

*Last night I heard all the songs from the opera Carmen. They're beautiful, but after all, look whose name it has!*

*Velma, my morale is awfully low. I have been receiving returned letters from Gene every day. I had mailed him a good luck coin and an important answer to a question he asked, and he never received it. It makes me feel terrible. Please ask Mom if she has a picture of Gene in his flying suit. I would like to have one. I think the one printed in the paper is very good of him.*

*My girlfriend's brother who was reported missing is now reported a prisoner. It hasn't been very long, since August.*

*Please don't forget to tell me if anything is wrong. All my love and luck to you whom I wish and would like to see soon.*

*Always,*

*Carmen*

*September 2, 1944*

*Dearest Vee,*

*Just received a wonderful letter from you. I adore that flower you traced.*

*I heard on the radio about the Russians giving liberty to some 1100 boys who were in prison camps. I do hope Gene was in one of them. I heard six boys say things about their experiences in the camps. They went through quite a bit, poor things.*

*Is Bob still in California? I do hope he doesn't go overseas. He's a very handsome boy, and you two make a very nice couple.*

*I went out to the woods to pick some wild flowers. I got a handful of golden rod. They're yellow and very beautiful. I always have some by Gene's picture and on the dining room table.*

*Forgive this scribbling but it's already late and I must hurry. I'll have to close now.*

*Adios muchacha linda,*

*Carmen*

Classes at Pratt & Whitney take Vee's mind off of the war. They have moved on to metallurgy. She tries to bring her grades back to some level of competency while allowing herself some fun on the job. When she and a coworker finish their required work early one evening, their supervisor tells them to "kill time as gracefully as possible." Instead, they play like a couple of children who have been pent up for days.

At Loretta and Ken's, the twins gear up for the start of school. Vee and Jeanie still spend most of their free time shopping or at the movies. She lets her friend talk her into the occasional double date, though she feels a pang of regret when she spots a young man who looks remarkably like Al.

Most disheartening is the fact that the letters she has been writing to her brother start coming back unopened. At the same time, her mother receives a number of responses to her queries of the other mothers and wives.

> *Pine Bluff, Arkansas*
> *September 2, 1944*
> *Dear friend, Mrs. Hammontree,*
>
> *Your welcome letter was received in today's mail in regard to our son, C. W. Nichols, missing since July 18 over Germany. We are sorry to say we have no further information regarding these boys. We did not know for sure any one of them had a chance to use his parachute until your letter arrived, and want to assure you we both feel better about it now. Your letter let us know more about the battle.*
>
> *We had a letter from the wife of the pilot of the plane. I believe she would be very glad to hear from you.*
>
> *The name of the town the boys were bombing at the time is "Memmingen" not far from the Swiss border. Perhaps some of them made it to Switzerland and are interned.*
>
> *We have hopes for all the boys to get out before long and return safe, as you know. Prayer, Hope, and Faith goes a long way helping them, so I take this means to thank you for your kind letter. Should we receive any word regarding any of the boys on the flight, we'll let you know at once. Hoping you receive good news very soon.*
>
> *Yours truly,*
> *Mr. and Mrs. Nichols*

> *Amarillo, Texas*
> *September 2, 1944*
> *Dear Mrs. Hammontree,*
>
> *I know you will be disappointed when I tell you I have no information of any kind concerning my husband Wright, except what you told me in your letter.*

*I just wanted you to know how much I appreciated your letter, as I hadn't had any word at all since I received the missing-in-action telegram. I didn't have any addresses of the crew members' families, therefore, I couldn't write to anyone. However, I have written to a friend of my husband's who is stationed in Italy. If I hear from him, I will let you know.*

*As near as I can check on it, some of the planes based in Italy bombed two German towns near the Swiss border. If that is where our husband and son went down, it could be possible they escaped into Switzerland. However, I don't have too much hope of that.*

*The Red Cross told me that if a person is interned in a neutral country, it is usually from three to six months before you get a report from the government. If you receive any additional information, I will appreciate it if you will let me know.*

*Sincerely,*

*Mrs. W. W. McGee*

*Valley Stream, New York*

*September 6, 1944*

*My dear Mrs. Hammontree,*

*Received your letter today and will try to answer it to the best of my knowledge. I am Richard's mother. My son was pilot of that plane. Up to this day, I have not had any other word or any information other than the telegram stating he has been missing since July 18 over Germany.*

*I had a letter from a friend of Richard's that was in a different squadron stating that sixteen planes were lost, and he thought that Richard was in one of those squadrons, but said he's sure they got out with their parachutes. So, my dear, that is all I can say, only that we must trust in God that our boys are safe and well, and I hope we will soon hear from them.*

*You see, Mrs. Hammontree, I have only the two sons, and I just got word today that my youngest son has arrived in Italy. They are two fine boys. I have been so heart-broken, lonesome and blue for them. And I know just how you feel, but we will not give up. God is good, and I know if we just put all our trust in him, he won't let us down.*

*My son Richard will be married one year on September 9th, and my heart goes out to his sweet little wife, but she too knows they are all right. I will let you know at once of any word, and I hope you will let me know.*

*Sincerely,*

*Mrs. M. Combs*

*Baltimore, Maryland*
*September, 1944*
*Dear Mrs. Hammontree,*

*I only wish I did have some more information to give you—but I know nothing except what you know. I, too, received a letter from the commanding officer in response to mine, and he told me exactly what you heard. His letter made me feel much, much better, though, particularly the part where he said the sky was filled with parachutes.*

*I am David's wife, and I have had the pleasure of meeting Gene and saw him quite often while we were in Tampa. Somehow I can't help but feel that they are all alright—and I think we can all be of great help to each other if we should hear anything further. I hope you will do this for me, and you can be sure I shall do the same. Even if I receive a wire that he is a prisoner, I will let you know because it is quite possible we may not all hear at the same time.*

*At least we know this war will be over soon—and if they are prisoners, the Nazi's won't have them long!!*

*Sincerely,*
*Mrs. David Blake*

The irony is not lost on Vee that, while the families are busy networking and exchanging information, a Lieutenant Oakley sends a letter to her father reiterating the same tired apologies and regretting that "the names of those who were in the plane and the names and addresses of their next of kin may not be furnished at the present time."

"So much for military security," Vee scoffs. When a second letter follows Lt. Oakley's, she notes "The military is nothing if not redundant."

*Fifteenth Air Force*
*10 September 1944*
*Dear Mr. Hammontree:*

*On 18 July 1944 heavy bombardment planes of this command attacked enemy installations at Memmingen, Germany. The Flying Fortress on which your son, Second Lieutenant Eugene L. Hammontree was navigator, failed to return from this raid.*

*I know that since you received the War Department's notice stating that your son is missing in action, you have been anxious to obtain further details. While we do not have complete information at hand, returning crews have reported that Eugene's formation was attacked by enemy fighter planes over the target. A severe battle ensued during which your son's ship was severely damaged. The stricken aircraft fell away from the others and soon passed from view in the clouds below the attacking force. Several parachutes were seen in the vicinity but at present it is impossible for us to predict whether Eugene escaped injury. You may be assured that if more detailed information becomes available, the War Department will notify you immediately.*

*America owes a debt that she can never repay to brave men like your son who, by their courage and skill, are bringing us closer to the final victory. I am sure that you are proud of Eugene, and I would like to have you feel that the members of this command share in your pride.*

*Very sincerely yours,*
*N. F. Twining*
*Major General, USA*
*Commanding*

# HOME FRONT

# TWENTY

**A**fter a month and a half of classwork, the Pratt and Whitney students are treated to a graduation ceremony. Vee receives orders to start working the night shift on gear assembly at the plant proper. She makes the eight-mile walk to fill out more paperwork and attend orientation. After a short evening nap, she returns to the plant at midnight to begin the task of supporting the war effort in earnest.

Dehydrating potatoes or labeling grease and oil were honest and necessary endeavors, but it was difficult to internalize how much it truly mattered. Building airplane engines, however, makes a deep connection for Vee, not just to the war, but to her brother and his safety. Gene is an airman. Bob will be flying soon. Pratt & Whitney provides the opportunity to pro-actively help any number of US servicemen return alive and, hopefully, unharmed.

Her parents deliver her winter clothes to Ken and Loretta's, and return home with her summer wardrobe for storage.

Bob continues to court his wife's affection by sending gifts. One contains a lovely silver heart-shaped compact. She shows it off at work where she and Marjorie use their new manufacturing knowledge to figure out what kind of finish it has.

"Looks like three different ones," Vee says.

"Polished, ground, and machined. We should hardness test it."

Vee pulls it back from the onlookers. "What? And ruin it?"

"At least let the crib man etch your name on it."

The idea intrigues Vee, so she considers having it monogrammed by a professional. At the jewelry store the next day, the owner asks what it's made of.

"Gee! That's one thing we forgot to do last night. Put it through metallurgy!" She turns it to the back and shows him the sterling silver stamp.

On her return home, Vee opens a letter from her mom writing that Gene's friend Claude Ament has died in the war. It is a blow to everyone's spirits.

Wayne has written, but he is hard-pressed to find something positive to say. He was in the third wave on Omaha Beach the day the allies stormed Normandy. Though his placement so far back in the surge saved his life, he felt the burden of the many bodies he had had to climb over to take the beaches. With living comes a certain amount of guilt. Each letter cuts away more and more of the abstract quality that is the hell of war. Like so many on the home front, Vee looks for distraction in the every day activities of movies and radio programs. As always, she is drawn into music.

*Tampa, Florida*
*September 14, 1944*
*Dearest Sis,*

*What a wonderful letter I received from you today. Don't you worry, you'll be my maid of honor if we have a church wedding. I wouldn't think of getting married without all of you attending. This morning's paper had a picture of a Missouri girl who married a boy from Tampa. Just think, some day I'll have my picture in the paper, but it'll be a Tampa girl and a Missouri boy, instead.*

*We bought a phonograph last week, and already have so many records we don't know what to do with them. We have Blue Danube, Skater's Waltz, Tonight We Love, and many others. I can't find Stardust anywhere. I looked all over town and still can't find it. I'll look until I do.*

*Just before I received the bad news about Gene, I was going to mail him a package. I still have it here wrapped. I found a large amount of chewing gum, so decided to send it to him. I do hope it doesn't turn to powder.*

*All my love to you,*

*Carmen*

As the workers adjust to their duties and relax around each other, work takes on much the same playfulness that Vee experienced at the Simplot plant in Idaho. When the machines operate at their finest, and the crews can relax a bit, they tease each other or taunt the supervisory crews. Not only is work more interesting than her previous factory jobs, but it's fun.

"I wonder why my hands are having such strange cramps," Vee says one evening.

"Couldn't be because you wrote a hundred salvage tickets, could it?" Bonnie asks. "Oh, by the way, I've been taking inventory."

"And?"

"There's only three good-looking men in the entire building."

At break, the one they nicknamed Tarzan comes into the room and is immediately swarmed by a group of women. Bonnie decides he isn't worth flirting with. "Too much competition."

The city is noisier than Caldwell, and the twins do not understand the need for quiet when they are home from school. Vee finds it harder to sleep during the days.

When she is home sick—which happens more often than it should—Loretta cares for her as if she is one of Loretta's own. When Vee worries about being a burden, Loretta brushes it off. "Don't give it a second thought." Vee returns the kindness by helping with washing and looking after the twins when she is not too tired.

In late September, Mildred receives a letter from Mrs. McGee saying her husband Wright has been listed as a prisoner of war. Additionally, Vee's cousin Dude is home on furlough. As positive as the news is, it sends a roller-coaster of emotions rippling through the family. Hope is such a tenuous thing. What Vee cannot do for her brother, she decides to do for Wayne. She buys a lovely card to include with the cookies she packages as a Christmas gift. She posts the box to Wayne and another to Bob.

*Tampa, Florida*
*September 20, 1944*
*Dearest Vee,*

*You make me very happy when you say that you are going to try again and make good with Bob. I bet it is a beautiful compact. Is it silver? I have seen some down here.*

*The planes down here have the cutest names such as "Flying Bananas," "King Koo," "Venus" and they have a picture representing the different names. They fly so low around here, it scares me to death at times.*

*I went shopping with Mother Saturday and saw a beautiful coat suit. I just had to have it. It's blue-gray and has three big buttons on the coat, and smaller buttons on the suit. It was $90, but I paid half and will keep paying until winter. I may need it if I get to go up there. It is cold there, isn't it? Does it snow? I haven't seen snow. I may sound silly, but I hear about the fun you have playing in the snow.*

*Now, with all that money you are making, you can spend some and still have some left to save. Don't do like I do. I start saving and when I go to town and see something pretty, I get it and there goes my money.*

*All my love,*
*Carmen*

Jeanie brings Dude to the city one afternoon, and the three of them wander from one end of town to the other. Dude is his old devil-may-care self, pushing the bounds of propriety while deftly avoiding any discussion of his war experience. Perhaps he is sensitive to Vee's circumstance, or perhaps his experiences are too raw for him to face. Either way, the trio manages to put war out of their minds for a while.

The twins celebrate their ninth birthday on September 28th. After the party, Loretta looks at Ken and says, "Nine years ago tonight, Ken was so excited he couldn't even cut wood to get supper with. He just sat on the woodpile with his mouth open and that far away look in his eyes."

"Yeah," Ken replies. "I was wondering *Good Lord! What have I done to deserve this?*"

Complain as he might, the love between them is palpable. It reminds Vee of the Corn family—comfortable and warm, mutual respect laced with humor.

A rumor begins to circulate of a strike at work. Vee believes wartime is not the time to fight over conditions or pay at the factory. "Isn't there enough fighting in the world? I sure hope they settle whatever they're feuding over." By the next night, the strike is called off.

*Tampa, Florida*
*October 1, 1944*
*Dearest Vee,*

*You can't realize how happy you make me when you say you're trying again with Bob. Just imagine when this terrible war is over, how nice it will be to be together again and think about a family. You do want children, don't you? It would be nice to have a little Velma and Bobbie.*

*The high schools are starting their football season. There was a game Friday, and I went with some girlfriends. The field where they played brought back memories as there's where I met dear Gene. They had a small carnival there at the time. Oh! What happy days. I'll never forget them as long as I live.*

*I'm awfully glad you like your job. Do you like to work at night? I couldn't work at night and sleep during the day. I guess you have to get accustomed to everything nowadays.*

*All my love and luck,*
*Carmen*

Bob writes to say he will be leaving Muroc Air Field in a few weeks, presumably heading into the Pacific theater. History is fraught with examples of countries failing to survive wars fought simultaneously on two fronts. It appears that Germany is losing ground in its efforts to do so. Vee wonders if the US forces can prevail under such stress.

# TWENTY-ONE

**V**ee grows accustomed to the night shift, pushing to keep her sleep schedule regular even on her days off. She sleeps more during the hours the twins are in school. When her friends want to see a movie on her nights off, she suggests the midnight showings. Still, she succumbs frequently to illness, especially her tonsils. A doctor's visit affirms that they will have to come out, eventually.

*France*

*Oct 9, 1944*

*Dear Velma,*

*I received two letters from you today along with twenty-seven others. I was sure glad o get them.*

*It will soon be a year since I got home last. I wish I was that close now. But who knows, I may be sometime. I sure hope you have heard from Eugene by this time and that he is alright. I hope Bill doesn't have to get mixed up in this mess. But I suppose he is like all of us were. Didn't know what it was all about till it was too late.*

*The show "Always in My Heart" is sure a swell picture. I saw it before I came to the Army at Lee Summit. I remember when we used to go to the show back home and it would be a murder picture. How you girls would cry.*

*I will close for this time. Write soon. Goodnight.*

*Love as ever,*

*Wayne*

At work, the antics continue. Boone sits at an adding machine one night and creates a mock paycheck for the crew.

"Gross pay – $99.99. Social Security – $1.20. War Bond – $18.75. Miscellaneous – $12.00. War Chest Fund – $6.00. Income Tax – $61.00. Check total – $1.04."

Vee leans over the desk. "Oh, but you forgot my insurance."

"Oh, yes." Boone makes another tabulation. "$1.07. You owe me three cents, please."

One October day, the mail holds a lovely surprise.

*Tampa, Florida*

*October 12, 1944*

*Dearest Vee,*

*Well, here is that picture I promised. It's not very good, but you have an idea what I look like. I sent another one to Mom. It's a different pose than yours. You said I never told what I looked like. Well, I have dark chestnut hair, brown eyes, and fair complexion. My hair is naturally curly. Gene would go crazy combing my hair.*

*How is Bob? You never tell me much about him anymore. The news is pretty good. I hope he doesn't have to go.*

*I hope we'll have a very good Christmas with the surprise of having Gene with us. When the postman comes by, I'm always anxious to hear from you and Mom about Gene.*

*A boy from Tampa was being held a prisoner but he escaped with fourteen others and is now on his way home. Isn't that grand?*

*Always,*

*Carmen*

Vee loves the photo. Carmen looks just as she pictured her—cute as a button, beautiful dark eyes, and a sweet sweet smile. The Missouri girl will be happy to stand up for the Tampa girl at the wedding. Something the two women share deeply—and Vee looks for in every letter—is her optimism that Gene will return safe. Still, the news from Carmen can be mixed.

*Tampa, Florida*
*October 21, 1944*
*Dearest Vee,*

*Wow! What a terrible hurricane we have been through. We were all scared to death. Our chicken coup landed across the street, and our citrus was ruined. Many of the shipyard workers' families had to take shelter in one of the school buildings. Thank goodness we didn't suffer more than we did. I'm sending you several paper clippings about the storm.*

*We have a lot of cleaning up to do, but thanks to our neighbor's help, we'll get through tomorrow or the day after. Besides the storm, there was a high number of fires caused by electric wires. One of the shipyard's warehouses was burned, and the loss is estimated at $20,000,000. So much for that.*

*Lots of love and luck,*
*Carmen*

The strongest wind Vee has ever experienced might have pushed the limits of fifty miles per hour. She cannot fathom what a hundred and thirty or more might be like. The destruction sounds horrid, and many of those who might help in the recovery are facing the winds of war so far from home. Vee pushes back against the fear by shutting out much of the war news. But life has a pernicious way of reminding her.

*Muscatine, Iowa*
*October 22, 1944*
*Dear Mrs. Hammontree,*

*In regards to your letter about my brother Mearl Danfeldt, we have had no further information other than that which you have already received.*

*I am very sorry, but I was unable to write sooner due to unfortunate circumstances. The day your letter came, I was taken to the hospital to await the birth of my baby, and I was there for two weeks. The baby was so small and weak, they had to keep him there for two more weeks. So, you can see, I have had plenty of worry.*

*My mother has been very worried also due to the fact that my younger brother has been sent overseas just recently, and that has just been an added worry. I hope we all hear good news soon.*

*I remain,*

*Mrs. Lanfier*

The Danfeldt brothers. The Combs brothers. It is difficult enough having one brother in harm's way. Vee is ever so grateful that Harold and Bill are too young yet. Hedrick is already talking about enlisting on his birthday.

As often as life weighs on her spirits, it lifts them to heights she has never imagined. Jeanie wakes her from a deep sleep one afternoon, insisting that she get dressed up.

"But I have work tonight!"

"Never mind that," Jeanie says, pushing hangers aside to find a proper outfit. "I have tickets. We're going to the Philharmonic!"

The concert is unimaginably beautiful—the clarity of tones, the perfect acoustics, the way the bass notes vibrate in her chest. The experience is as physical as it is cerebral, and it moves her to tears.

The concert inspires the girls to attend the Oscar Levant piano recital at the Music Hall the following Saturday, but when they arrived, the lines are already long, and people are being turned away. They settle for listening to scratchy records or the tinny second-hand concerts on the radio which are now littered with ads for the upcoming presidential election. Vee is tired of hearing the same ads repeat "and that's why we need change" or "agayn agayn and agayn."

When the sun plays through the fall clouds, the two friends walk the city or spent a lazy afternoon at Swope Park. The money in their pockets never stays hidden for long. Vee amasses stacks of the latest sheet music and often buys Hallmark cards instead of plain stationery. She purchases fabric and patterns and, with Loretta's help, sews new clothes every few weeks. More and more, she finds the courage to spend her money on ready-mades off the racks. She makes good money at the plant, and for the first time in her life, she refuses to "just get by."

On limited sleep, she stumbles to work one night and finds everyone in a mean mood. The vending machine has been stocked with Hershey brand chocolate instead of the cheaper brand they have had to put up with. Her coworkers are elated until they realized they will have to buy two packages of licorice sticks to get one Hershey bar. Vee eats her fill of licorice.

Pratt & Whitney sends out letters to the workers asking that if anyone happens to see "idle men" around—preferably able-bodied—sign them up to work at P&W.

"If you find any of those," Loretta says while ironing, "put them under lock and key!"

In late October, Wayne writes a letter which eased her mind. There seems to be little of the weight of war in his words, though she knows he has learned to censor his own writings just as Gene has.

*France*
*October 27, 1944*
*Dear Vee,*

*I've been trying to write to the folks back home, but it seems like nothing happens over here that they will let a guy write about.*

*I bet you have a time when you take care of the twins. They really give their ideas on the way things should go.*

*I get kinda disgusted at these darn French people over here. If you can't understand what they are saying, you don't know whether they are talking sensible or whether they are cussing you. Sometimes I expect they do cuss us. Sometimes I think I am in Holland. Almost all of these people wear wooden shoes.*

*I sure wish I could have been home when Dude was there. I bet we would have tore the town apart. But just wait till we do get back home.*

*The other day, a French woman came up here and wanted to trade us a chicken for something to eat. We traded some K ration biscuits. Yesterday, one of the boys said he would pick it and clean it if I would fry it. I made gravy, too. It was pretty good if I did cook it myself.*

*Goodnite. Write soon.*

*Lots of love as ever,*

*Wayne*

*Tampa, Florida*

*November 1, 1944*

*Dearest Vee,*

*What beautiful weather we're having. It's nice and sunny every day. Of course, it's cool in the mornings and evenings.*

*The Ford ran out of gas this morning, and we had to push it for five blocks. Wow! What a job, and no man helped us.*

*I received a letter and Gene's picture from Mom yesterday. Also a letter from Harold. He's so cute.*

*I read in the paper where the 15th Air Force in Italy is celebrating their first birthday. Maj. Gen. Nathan Twining is doing a very good job.*

*Time has come for me to close. I must write to Mom and dear little Harold.*

*"Short but Sweet"*

*Carmen*

On Tuesday, November 7th, several of Vee's coworkers catch a ride with Boone who drives them to their various precincts before dropping them at their homes. The country has already been arguing over the legal age to vote—the idea that eighteen-year-olds are old enough to fight and die for their country and should be able to vote—but all Vee can do is watch the process unfold around her. She will turn nineteen in December, still two years too young to have a voice at the polls. That does not stop her from having an opinion.

"O Happy Day! Roosevelt is elected for a fourth term!"

When she travels to Harrisonville on weekends, Vee spends an occasional night with her in-laws. Those evenings, she finds herself missing her husband. She adores Bob's mother and his sister Norma who is serious about her own boyfriend, Charles. The two girls start their Christmas lists—shopping and helping each other decide. "Do your Christmas hinting early," she tells her sister-in-law with a wink.

For Vee, her birthday and Christmas run together most years—only three days apart. It is seldom that she is treated as special as this year when a package arrives from Bob. His note reads, "Darling, with this comes three wishes: Happy Birthday, Merry Christmas, and a Happy New Year. Love, Bob."

She opens the box to find a beautiful Bulova wristwatch like she has never dreamed of owning. Gold and dainty, with a black band. She cannot believe it is hers. Immediately, she pens a note saying how much she loves that little message.

At work, she keeps forgetting about her new watch and asks Hudson for the time more than once. Boone accuses her of simply wanting everyone to notice.

*Los Angeles*
*Nov 11, 1944*
*Dear Velma,*

*It's too hot here and I'm starved. I'm gnawing on a chocolate bar which must be composed of the ingredients used in the cement in front of Grauman's Chinese Theater—it wouldn't melt if you held it over a fire.*

*Guess you've had no word of Gene yet or we'd have heard the good news. Did you ever play a Ouija Board? We asked it about Gene and of course you can't believe what it said, but its answer was "injured leg – getting some care in enemy territory by private family" or words to that effect. If such were true, he couldn't get a letter out of the country to let anyone know he was safe. He'd be caught for sure.*

*Things are pretty lively around here. Still go to USO and on Sunday afternoons there are dances at Earl Carroll's supper club for the servicemen.*

*We have "hen parties" a lot because of a "man shortage" – Dolores and Mary and a neighbor girl Donna and I. Donna is quite a talented writer. One radio script she wrote was put on a recording but don't know what will come of it. Are you doing any more writing since school? It's so simple to write in school but boy when you wait for the spirit to move you or for an inspiration, 'its' a lot different. I doubt if I'd ever be a prolific writer.*

*I guess this takes care of the news for now. Hello to everyone when you see them.*

*Love,*

*Sophia Barbara*

They still have no word about Gene. As much as she loves her connection with Carmen, she feels the constant reminder of what might not come to pass wears on her mother. Mildred writes to Carmen less frequently. And when Vee reads that her little brother Harold is taking up the correspondence, she sends a note of caution that Carmen does not receive well.

*Tampa, Florida*

*November 11, 1944*

*Dear Vee,*

*I'm awfully angry at you for saying what you said in your last card. You know I love to hear from all of you. It makes me feel, well, as if I'm loved by all of you. Please don't tell Harold Dean to stop writing to me. He writes so much like Gene, it makes me feel good to receive a letter from him.*

*Those post cards you've been sending are really beautiful. I can't wait to see all those interesting places.*

*We had a very nice parade early this morning. Joe marched in it with his new ROTC uniform. He really looked grand. Just think, all those school boys will make good soldiers of tomorrow.*

*I'm having an awful time getting some gas for the car. We're entitled to only three gallons, and that doesn't take us anywhere. We live six and a half miles from town, and that takes quite a bit of gas. I hoped we wouldn't have any more rationing! It's a headache. Can you find any butter? We have to make our own. It's a good thing we have a cow. We have some to spare and give some to the soldier's wife next door. They just moved in Tuesday last week. She's just a kid and is awfully sweet.*

*I have to pick some oranges that are ripe, so must hurry and close. Dad's calling for me.*

*Love always,*

*Carmen*

# TWENTY-TWO

**N**ot only does Vee enjoy her job, but she's good at it. By mid-November, she puts out sixty gears a night. Kier, Boone, Hudson and the other women at the plant have become a second family. So much so, that everyone feels the blow when they find Sadie in a locker room one night, crying her eyes out. Her husband Jack is missing in the Pacific.

The news hits Vee hard as she thinks of Bob. He has not written in over a week. Every night, someone on the crew shares a story of family or friends who have gone missing or are killed, and every day, Vee watches the post for some reassurance from her husband. She stops waiting for word from Gene. It will happen when the time was right.

For Christmas, she decides to buy Bob a wedding ring to match hers. She chooses an engraving for the inside, and finds a leather address book as a second gift. Still no word from Bob. When the phone rings one evening, she bawls out Jeanie for scaring her to death.

"I thought I was about to get the kind of call that Sadie got!"

Thankfully, Bob writes two days later. The euphoric relief dies when Bob sends another letter with a new photo of himself in uniform. It is a good likeness except for his eyes. Something about them haunts her, reminding her of how much he has changed. There are stories of men changed by combat, but Bob has not seen real fighting yet.

The plant runs shifts through Thanksgiving Day, and, rather than making a harried run to Harrisonville and back, Vee plans to have her holiday meal with Kier and Millie.

"The meal was swellelegant!" Vee says after stuffing herself with roast duck, green beans, corn, celery, radishes, backed apples, cake and cranberries. Hudson joins them later before they catch some sleep ahead of night shift.

On her first Sunday off in weeks, Vee spends the day with Loretta and the twins at the Nelson-Atkins Museum of Art. Nothing in her past has prepared her for the array of beautiful paintings and sculptures, or for the grandeur of the building itself. Each time she looks a little deeper, Kansas City reinvents itself, drawing her in with its cultural offerings. She can hardly imagine moving back to the country and to rural farm life.

Christmas approaches, and tensions build at work. Kier and Hudson start fighting over nothing. Everyone misses Boone who is reassigned to day shift. The cold weather does not help.

"Earl gave blood last week. The cold weather has persuaded him to go get it back!"

Carmen sends a very somber letter.

*Tampa, Florida*
*November 30, 1944*
*Dearest Vee,*

*I received a letter from Mom yesterday, and I'm writing you before answering her. Things have been happening around here lately. My girlfriend's little brother was drowned. He missed his school bus, and on his way home, started playing in a water hole. He got on a board, but it turned over and he fell in. They found him that night. That family has had the worst luck.*

Melinda B Hipple

*There was also a terrible accident in one of our shipyards. An iron plank fell and mashed four men flat. There was another one seriously injured, and they're expecting him to die. It's terrible to meet death in that way.*

*I heard on the radio this morning where people bought 14 million dollars worth of bonds in Kansas City. Keep up the good work, kid. Any time I hear anything concerning Missouri, I listen to it as if it were my own hometown.*

*This Christmas will be a miserable one for me. No news from Gene, and not knowing what he's going through.*

*There's much more I would want to write, but "time waits for no one."*

*Love, luck,*

*Carmen*

November 30th brings the first snow of winter in Kansas City. It is easier to ride the streetcars to work than for Hudson to navigate her usual carpool route. The weather slows production, but P&W's front office still compliments third shift on their quality of work and their numbers. As they clear the top shelf of product to be etched, first shift wonders why they have not dusted it while they are up there.

Bob is finally shipping out and says not to write to his California address. The next step will be an APO which means he could be anywhere in the world. Anywhere in combat. When he tries calling Vee directly, she answers the phone, but all she can hear is him talking to the operator. He cannot hear her. At one point, the operator tells him the line is busy.

"Well, of course it's busy," Vee complains. "I'm on it!"

She tries calling back, but is told that Bob has returned to camp. As is common, by the time she finishes with a long-distance call, she does not have a civil tongue left.

To clear her head, she takes a walk in the fresh snow. Streets usually blackened by soot and grime sparkle under the purifying white. The beauty of it puts her in the mood to shop for Christmas gifts. Afterwards, she tunes in to an opera which helps clear her mind. But it is a letter forwarded from home that lifts her spirits the most.

*Amarillo, Texas*
*December 4, 1944*
*Dear Mr. and Mrs. Hammontree,*

*I have thought of you so much lately and have wondered if you have heard any news concerning your son, Eugene.*

*I have been notified that Wright is a German prisoner of war. I am so happy and relieved. I only hope you have been notified your son is safe.*

*I also have received word that this raid of July 18 was one of the outstanding raids of the war. Those in the second group were awarded the "Presidential Citation."*

*I want you to know that, as I pray for Wright each night, I remember Eugene. May they all be safe and return to us soon.*

*Sincerely,*
*Mrs. W. W. McGee*

The only gift more uplifting would be if Gene himself walked through her door. At last, the family has definitive word that someone from his plane survived.

The news bolsters her productivity at work. The entire team rises to the occasion, setting a record number of gears to "finished stores" for the night. Out of five inspectors—with only three actually inspecting—they make seventy-one gears per person when the company requires a minimum of ten. Their success is not just about the team. Each member feels pride in their accomplishment as if they are fighting a war front of their own.

And then a second of Gene's crew members is reported alive and in captivity.

*Bethlehem, Pennsylvania*
*December 14, 1944*
*My Dear Mr. Hammontree,*

*We received your name and address from the government. Our son, Russell Becker, was the belly turret gunner on their ship.*

*I hope you have heard from Eugene and that he is in good health and not injured. Our son has not had such good fortune. He has had both his legs injured. Mrs. McGee said her husband was also wounded, and that a bomb fell short of its target while they were aboard a prison train. Russell has been imprisoned at Stalag Luft 4 at Belgard, Germany.*

*It certainly has been a comfort to write to the parents whose sons served with our son. They certainly must have been a good crew. May God protect them and speed the day of their homecoming.*

*Yours respectfully,*

*Mr. and Mrs. Becker*

*Tampa, Florida*

*December 20, 1944*

*Dearest Vee,*

*I was rudely interrupted by the phone last night. A lonesome M.P. wanted to talk to someone. He just dialed our number. Boy oh boy, did I tell him where to get off. They think they can get anyone with their line. Of course, there are some good and some bad, like in everything else.*

*Thank you very much for that beautiful card. What I would give to see some snow. I hope to do so in the near future, just as soon as Gene takes me there. I know he'll show up. What a lucky day for all of us.*

*I'm so blue tonight. I'm blue quite often, anymore. I see a pretty scene, I cry like a fool. Whenever I hear a pretty song, I cry. And now, when I hear Christmas carols, I cry. There is one song that makes me cry awful when I hear it—I'll Be Home for Christmas. I really shouldn't do that as it's just a song.*

*I was thinking, you could call me up and talk to me before Christmas. I'll find out the rates and tell you about it. The number is H45-622.*

*Love, love, love always,*

*Carmen*

At dinner break in the early morning of December 21st, the girls at P&W shower Vee with birthday cards and new, delicate hankies.

"Who told you?" she asks in total surprise.

Everyone looks at Hudson who holds out the cutest cupcake with pink frosting. Kier used a toothpick to engrave "Happy Birthday" into it.

Nor has Loretta forgotten. She gives Vee a photo of their family and a ladies undershirt for the cold winter ahead.

Her mom comes later in the day—a rare surprise for Mildred to travel all the way into the city. She gives her daughter a beautiful card and a new diary for the coming year.

In her old diary—quickly dwindling down to only a handful of blank pages—Vee writes, "Happy Birthday to me. 'Ain't' I the egotistical one, tho?!"

Before she can blink, the holiday arrives. The plant closes for the long weekend, so Vee rides to Harrisonville with Loretta and Ken on Saturday.

She sleeps through Sunday services as is her habit now. Through the day, she plays the organ, reads through the cards and letters her parents have received, and plays with Wiggles—her parents' dog. The tiny puppy has grown into a stout little rat terrier, mostly white with black accessories. His stub of a tail wags every time Vee looks at him.

Christmas Day tradition in the Hammontree home starts with breakfast. As soon as everyone has eaten their fill of scrambled eggs, and biscuits and gravy, they settle around the cedar tree Trucil cut from the back acres and Mildred decorated with paper chains and store-bought tinsel.

Harold Dean receives a diary and a pair of leather gloves. Bill, leather gloves. And Hedrick, a white scarf. Aunt Irene sent fruitcake. They receive candy from their dad. Her mom gives Vee a coveted pair of hose—hard to find in wartime. She also receives bath salts from Hedrick, stationery from Harold, and Tea Rose from Bill. As the only girl, her brothers tend to spoil her.

Jeanie's gift to Vee contains a pair of the softest white fur mittens. Betty Corn sent Apple Blossom powder and a beautiful powder mitt to apply it with. Carmen gifts Vee an address book covered in a delicate floral fabric. Only one thing would make the day more perfect. She quietly hopes the Germans let the prisoners celebrate Christmas in their own way.

*Tampa, Florida*
*Christmas*
*Dearest Vee,*

    *Thank you ever so much for the roses. They were already dead, but they were beautiful anyway. I got a quilted robe, a pair of winter pajamas (they know I will need them later), two pair of silk stockings (boy they are precious, we can't get any down here), and a pair of solid gold earrings from my dad. Oh, and a box of stationery from your mom and dad. I'm now using it, of course. You are the first to get to see it.*

    *We always have celebrated Christmas, but not this year. All the boys are having a bad time and me not knowing about Gene. It wouldn't be fair. Today our club, (the old maid's club) consisting of only six girls whose husbands or boyfriends are overseas, are going to have dinner and then to a movie.*

    *How is Bob? Has he gone overseas yet?*
*Love always,*
*Carmen*

Vee works the 26th without having slept much in two days. At one point, she falls asleep near Sadie in the locker rooms. When Sadie wakes, she asks, "Did you have a nice Christmas?"

"Yeah, only it's ending pretty lousy, isn't it?"

Sadie responds with a quiet, "Yeah."

"Still no word about Jack?"

"No. Still no word about Gene?"

They go back to the line and work diligently until about 5:00 a.m. when Vee becomes violently ill.

"I could die and be thankful," she says when Kier comes to the locker room.

"You should go home. You're no good here, anyway."

Vee stays in bed for two days. Though she doesn't get much sleep, she rests enough to return to work. As she's reading a letter from her mother-in-law on her way home from the post office, Vee's knees buckle. Mrs. B apologizes for not seeing Vee over the holiday, but they, too, had been sick.

Aside from work, Vee stays in most of the week leading up to the New Year. She reads from her new purchase *The Collected Works of Edgar A. Guest* just so she can drool over it every so often. News from the European front sounds more positive, but that is little comfort. Bob is still in the States on Christmas Day, but is ready to leave on a moment's notice.

"Well, Diary, it looks like the last page. I'm kinda sorry, too. Forty-four has certainly been eventful for me. Gee, I would like to have gone out and really banged up a celebration tonight. Bye, Diary."

She closes the book and heads to work.

# TWENTY-THREE

**If the rest of the city celebrates the New Year, P&W's midnight shift hears none of it.** Instead, Mr. Lane treats them to a scolding on the subject of their "carelessness about getting enough sleep, talking too much, getting the measurements, and being AWOL." Vee knows the last part is aimed directly at her. Even though she has been legitimately ill, her missed days affect her rating which reflects badly on Lane's department.

But Vee's illness flares again and, despite Mr. Lane's warning, she spends another night AWOL from work. In the morning, her throat hurts so badly she can barely open her mouth. When she does, Loretta exclaims, "Good Lord! Your tonsils have plum met in the middle!"

Bob calls from Sacramento, and this time the two of them manage a five-minute conversation. He has no idea when or where he will be. Advances in Europe do not translate to the Pacific theater.

After the phone call, Loretta takes Vee's temperature.

"A hundred and two."

She misses work a second night in a row.

Feeling guilty that Loretta spends so much time fussing over her, Vee decides to help catch up on the family's ironing. An hour into the task, she notices something odd on her arms.

"Look! Ironing has made my measles pop out again! I've had these dern things twice before. Don't see why it was necessary to have them again."

Loretta confirms the spots and sends Vee to bed once more. She cooks hot soup for her patient and, later, plays *Many Happy Returns of the Day* on the piano to cheer her up.

"Mr. Lane will want to fire me."

"Nonsense. How could he fire one of his best workers?"

Saturday evening, the family sees a movie while Vee convalesces at home and listens to FDR's State of the Union speech. His words are uplifting and powerful, urging Americans to give everything they have for a victory against Nazi tyranny. He praises General Eisenhower for his steady command of the forces in Europe and makes special mention of the Allied forces in Italy—forces Gene had once been a part of. But his resolve to begin massive air offenses against Japan sends an uncontrollable shiver through Vee. Bob will be part of that offensive.

Roosevelt speaks of the need for more nurses. Vee admires nurses more than any other woman save Mrs. Roosevelt herself. And when FDR mentions the need for more workers in the factories that produced war goods, Vee nods her head and acknowledges to the air that she is doing her part.

Because of her illness, Vee misses a full week of work. She is happy to be back, though Mr. Lane does not speak to her the entire first night. After the president's speech, and with a renewed sense of progress in Europe, the girls fall into their duties with urgency. That does not stop them from driving Lane a bit loopy with their antics. As long as they keep their production numbers and inspections up—and they were putting out nearly a hundred parts apiece each night—he simply scowls at them from a distance.

"I haven't worn a dress in so long," Kier says when Lane moves out of earshot, "I'm not sure I'd even like them anymore."

Boone gives her shoulders a little shimmy. "I wore slacks back in the days when other women would turn around and call me a hussy!"

"I bet those same dames are wearing them now," Vee says, laughing at the thought.

*Tampa, Florida*
*January 6, 1945*
*Dearest Vee,*

*What a surprise! Two letters from you, just like old times when we both had more time.*

*Went to see Thirty Seconds Over Tokyo and cried all the way through. I was thinking about Gene, of course. Those boys went through a lot when they had the crash landing in the sea. It was just like the things that happened to Gene except he didn't lose his leg (thank God), and he didn't come back to the States. It really was a good movie.*

*Dad and three other men are trying to put in a sink and a new gas stove. They're really having some trouble as the old stove is over 500 pounds, and they can't carry it out. We had an awful time getting the new stove. I had to go to the rationing board and fill out several applications, then after some three weeks we got a slip to get another one.*

*I guess you have already heard about the three German spies that escaped from a Florida camp. They were captured yesterday. They had been through Tampa and tortured many families, occupying their home while away to a movie. We were all very worried but knew they couldn't come around our neighborhood as the camp is so close by. I better not see a German spy around me. I'll shoot him like a mad dog. Forgive me for talking like this, but I hate them terribly.*

*Gene gave me a large picture a week before he left. This month will make a year since I've known him. I went to Savannah to see him before he left the States on March 1st, but I was two hours late. You can imagine how bad I felt.*

*I don't think I've told you about our future trip to Havana, Cuba. I can't wait to go. We're leaving sometime in June or July for about three weeks. I'll send you something pretty from there.*

*Love, Luck, Always,*
*Carmen*

Bob begins sending letters through an APO address which means he is somewhere in the South Pacific. He writes regularly, but keeps his specific location censored. Vee purchases a handsome leather billfold as an anniversary gift. It is the first new one he has had in a while, and Vee hears that, where he is stationed, leather does not hold up long.

To dampen the shenanigans on third shift, Lane posts new rules.

"Makes the U.S. Constitution look like a short short story," Vee complains. "He hates me, even though I'm the fastest inspector on night shift. Why can't he just let us do our jobs?" She lets it be known that her highest product count now stands at 170 gears.

"Maybe it's because you're too good an aim with a paper wad."

Vee giggles. "The timekeeper wants me to take aim at Lane some time after the whistle blows. She's dared me."

Ken has news of his own. He is moving to second shift at the armory. Loretta calculates in her head and concludes that, between the twins, her husband's second shift, and Vee's third shift, she will have to make a meal every two hours and twenty minutes in order to feed everyone at the proper times.

The family sits down to a surprise at dinner—fresh sausage. "My father murdered a pig," Loretta informs them. "That's one way to get around the rationing." Each one at the table chews a little slower as they savor the rich taste of pork and spices.

On January 29th, Loretta wakes Vee at 9:30 in the evening, and on the dining table sits a card and a small white cake with one burning candle.

"It's a hell of an anniversary," Vee says, "celebrating alone."

Loretta smiles sweetly. "But you're not alone, dear."

\*\*\*

Mid-February brings another snow, but by this time, Vee is weary of delays and missed buses, and trudging through the muck. She travels to her parents for the weekend, but after they pick her up from town, her father parks the car at the highway and makes them walk the mile to the house. At least in the city, the trolley cars come within a couple of blocks of Loretta's.

Inside, Vee soaks up the heat from the fireplace as her dad throws another log on the fire. He tells her about the new house he is designing to be built just yards away, a concrete-block home that will be much roomier and more efficient. The log home will serve as a barn to house hay and chickens.

Mildred cooks a ham and serves it with scalloped potatoes, tomatoes, and canned plums.

After dinner, Trucil lays in another log which sends a crackle of sparks up the flue. Satisfied it will burn through the night, he pulls his fiddle from its case and rosins the bow—Vee's cue to pick up a guitar. They play a number of square-dance standards, easy to follow. Mildred rocks to the beat.

When Vee returns to the city the next day, she walks to Jenkins Music and purchases a number of popular and semi-classical songs—*Indian Love Call*, a Strauss waltz, *Always in My Heart*—adding to the stack of music her dad does not approve. But it is, after all, her own hard-earned money, and the city has opened her mind to a new world.

Bob is now stationed in the Marianas Islands somewhere in the south Pacific which sends Vee thumbing through Loretta's world atlas. Bob writes that he is a gunner and mentions that he has already flown one mission. With a stake in building aircraft, she wants to know if he flies on a B-29 or a B-17.

"Probably the 29," she thinks.

He sends a dazzling white scarf with an emblem in one corner and writing in the Hawaiian language. "Better find out what it means before you wear it," Loretta warns.

Bob's mother writes retelling his experiences bombing Iwo Jima. Vee wonders why he did not share the news with her.

"I certainly hopes he sinks it," she tells Sadie at work.

"Me, too. I want this horrid war to be done."

The girls sip coffee while they wait for midnight shift to start.

"I have news."

Vee perks up. "Good or bad?"

"Both. Jack showed up unexpectedly today. He's been released from duty."

"Oh, Sadie, that's great, isn't it?"

Sadie sets her cup down and reaches for Vee's hand. "I'm going home for a week so I can file for a divorce."

The news stuns Vee. The entire night shift has waited on pins and needles to hear Jack's status. She remembers Carmen's entreaties to make things work with Bob. She is trying, but it is not her place to say the same to Sadie. She merely squeezes her hand and offers an understanding nod.

During the shift, hardly anyone speaks to one another. Kay has been mad at Sadie since the party at Monty's. Martha will not eat because she and Ann are not getting along. Walsh appears to be mad at everyone. Perhaps it is the weather, but Vee wonders how much more these women can handle worrying about their loved ones, their friends, and each other. And if some women find their husbands changed by the war, others find themselves changed by their own experiences. The days and nights seem wrapped in a terrible limbo.

*War Department*

*1 March 1945*

*Dear Mr. Hammontree:*

*I am again writing you concerning your son, Second Lieutenant Eugene L. Hammontree, who was previously reported missing in action since 18 July 1944. It distresses me to have to inform you that no report of any change in his status has yet been received. If, at the expiration of twelve months, a missing person has not been accounted for, all available information regarding the circumstances attending his disappearance is reviewed under the provisions of Public Law 490, 77th Congress, as amended, at which time a determination of his status is made. Before the twelve months' period has elapsed, all data or evidence obtainable from any source which may be of any significance in the case is carefully considered. Occasionally, relatives and friends of missing personnel receive communications containing pertinent and reliable information not officially reported to the War Department. If you have received any such communications and will send them or photostatic copies of them to this office, it will be greatly appreciated. After their review, they will be returned to you if you so desire.*

*The War Department is mindful of the anguish you have so long endured and you may rest assured that, without any further request on your part, you will be advised promptly if any additional information concerning your loved one is received. Should it become necessary to establish his status in accordance with the provisions of the law cited, you will be notified of the findings shortly after the expiration of the twelve months' absence.*

*You have my heartfelt sympathy in your sorrow, and it is my earnest hope that the fortitude which has sustained you in the past will continue through this distressing period of uncertainty.*

*Sincerely yours,*

*J. A. Ulio*

*Major General*

*The Adjutant General*

# HOME FRONT

# TWENTY-FOUR

**V**ee's cousin, Sophia Barbara, has a beautiful singing voice. She has won a number of vocal competitions and has performed in school and community plays. Her talent seems destined for something bigger than Kansas City, so her family has moved to Los Angeles in the hopes she can pursue a career in Hollywood. She writes Vee a sixteen-page letter detailing her experiences—having a photographic portfolio taken, making audition records, and her first experience singing on the radio.

*Hollywood, California*
*Feb 22, 1945*
*Dear Velma,*

*The boss at this company, a wealthy so-and-so, asked me at Christmas to accompany him to a very ultra fur shop on Wilshire and model some minks so he could choose one for his wife. It was really a thrill dragging those luscious minks on and off. He asked my advice, me being quite the connoisseur of minks, you can imagine! He chose a beauty. Wanted to repay me, ha. A wolf, no doubt.*

# HOME FRONT

*Tonight, Mary and I are going to a USO lecture on psychology regarding the returning servicemen. They are planning more hospital tours and entertainments*

*Funny about measles – you can always catch them again under another adjective.*

*Things have been slow around here for me lately. I did send some poetry to a couple of places back east, and so far they haven't even bothered to send me a rejection slip let alone return my stuff. It's been at least three weeks.*

*You asked about my radio experience, but I wouldn't know where to start—whether you meant mic experiences or the characters I know. The latter far outshines the microphone. One old reprobate I worked for could write the most inspirational stuff if you'd just lock him up with a typewriter and a Bible. He wrote the series "Living Bible' which I played in, got to owing money, disappeared and was living on somebody's houseboat or yacht, then really vanished owing me $75 and others much more than that. Afra tried to locate him for us, and if he ever shows up in this country on any Afra station, he'll be banned from the air. He's definitely blacklisted. He used to have a very bohemian existence and I'd never go to any of his "parties."*

*No doubt I told you the "studio apartment" where Laura and I lived was done over from a barroom in this big old house which had been a restaurant. The handyman was a dope fiend who had a couple of "assistants" and they'd all get down in the furnace room below our apartment and mutter. A violinist and a soprano lived in the basement apartments and practiced there till the neighbors practically threatened their lives. Then a lady with a loquacious parrot moved in and it screamed "Ethel" the live-long day. The rest of the house was filled with artists, models, actors and occasionally a showgirl on tour. Mother shudders at some of the tales I've told her like not having a lock on our door for several weeks. She doesn't think much of my "characters" either, and I guess they don't sound very safe, but they were very colorful. There was a stairway that wound up through the center to the third floor. Whenever there was any disturbance on the first floor, they would all pop out their doors and hang over the stairway. It was a very funny sight. One night the "handyman" and another got into a fight over something right outside our door and screamed "murder" as he ran out into the snow. We finally peered out cautiously and met that stairway full of people gazing down curiously. Another time, Laura went into the hall to see why our refrigerator wasn't connecting and she blew a fuse. All the electricity went off and she screamed bloody murder. Everybody came thundering down the stairs. Later, I asked why she screamed and she showed me a black thumb and finger. She had received quite a shock.*

*We had to move as the place kept getting dirtier and they let people freeze or threaten their lives before they'd bother with the heat.*

*A lot of the actors would throw their money around whenever they got a good contract. Then sell expensive jewelry and stuff when they were out of work, and lead an entirely different life. One fellow had two Duesenbergs and a good American made car, too. Another used to have his limousine and chauffeur and wolfhound call for him after he got off "First Nighter" each week. Some of the actors lived in nice modern apartments a few blocks from the bohemian neighborhood. I finally moved into an apartment building to a more prosaic but more sanitary life.*

*The man who wrote the Bible program also wrote a gag show and commercials and spot announcements. Quite often I'd sit in on the meetings when the gag writers got together to hash over a program. It would go on and on and we'd lose track of time and everybody was full of ideas. Even me. The razzing and impromptu clowning that went on was usually funnier than the radio script they were trying to write. They'd order indigestible stuff from the drugstore most of the time and I envy neither their stomachs nor their poor wives.*

*Got a letter from John with the special services outfit at the University in Virginia, and he was talking about doing some hospital shows and other shows with Red Skelton who is a private in the army. He got a big kick out of it and thinks Skelton is an OK guy and a scream. John is just as funny, I think, and someday should go far. John used to live in this bohemian place I was telling you about. We often exchange tales about the place. He also was stationed in New York in January and saw five big Broadway shows as a guest of the Shuberts and attended a party at the Shubert's penthouse. Some fun!*

*Well, this is getting too long so will close. Have you seen Aunt Ella lately? Tell everybody down there hello for all of us.*

*Love,*

*Sophia Barbara*

Perhaps that is the inspiration for the pair of three and a half inch heelless, toeless, black patent leather shoes Vee buys. She sets them on the floor near her bed before trying to sleep. But the shoes call to her, repeatedly. She thinks of how lovely they look and peers at them over the edge of the bed. Of course, Bob will approve, but she toys with the idea of turning other heads.

She talks Hudson into spending Sunday with her at the art museum. Vee dresses in her suit and slides on the new shoes. It is a lovely day immersed in culture and surrounded by affluent homes in neighborhoods that dwindle off to forest nearer 64th Street.

Sadie returns to work that night.

"Did you file for divorce?"

"Oh, no. I just couldn't. He was so sweet to me." She shows off the new ring Jack brought her from India—a moonstone center and two light pink stones on either side.

"It's beautiful," Vee says, comparing it to her own modest ring.

"It will have to be my engagement ring, now," Sadie says. "My other one is at the bottom of the sea!"

The crew moves on from the real and imagined slights as the team comes back together. Vee brakes her own record and manages to put out over 200 gears that night.

***

Wayne writes to Loretta and assures everyone that he is okay. He is stationed in a relatively safe area, cooking and pulling guard duty. He still complains about the French not speaking proper English.

Lane's frustration and anger with night shift grows more bothersome every week. Rumors are that they might be getting a new supervisor. Everyone hopes it's true.

*Tampa, Florida*
*March 3, 1945*
*Dearest Vee,*

*Mary, our neighbor, is getting married tomorrow at 5 o'clock. Her boyfriend was overseas with Gene and in his same squadron. He doesn't remember him though. She hadn't seen him for three years, and there were periods of three months without hearing from him. He was telling me last night how he had to stay in a trench for three weeks with only K rations as the Jerries were over them all that time. He saw a lot of things that he doesn't want to ever see again as long as he lives. All of those boys are going through a lot.*

*As I've told you before, our club is composed of girls (over 24 now) whose boyfriends are in the service. We're doing quite a bit of Red Cross work. They're going to publish our picture in the paper, and as soon as they do, I'll send you a copy.*

*Vee, this will have to be all, so please answer soon.*

*Love,*

*Carmen*

*Kansas City Quartermaster Depot*

*March 8, 1945*

*Dear Mr. Hammontree:*

*The Army Effects Bureau has received and is forwarding to you some property belonging to your son, Second Lieutenant Eugene L. Hammontree.*

*The property is transmitted in order that you may safely keep it on behalf of the owner, pending change in his status. In the event he is later reported as a casualty, the property should be distributed according to the laws of the state of his legal residence. I sincerely hope that such distribution will not be necessary.*

*Yours very truly,*

*F. A. Eckhardt*

*Captain Q.M.C.*

*Assistant*

As the weather warms, Vee takes advantage of every musical, movie, and theatrical event she can. When no one is available to go along, she takes herself out on the town. Jeanie is inspiration for the courage and determination to take charge of her own life. Otherwise, she might have missed Helen Hayes' stunning performance in the role of Harriet Beecher Stowe.

"I'll always remember that chuckle down in her throat," she says later, "that clever humor, and the entrancing—yes, that's it—entrancing way she'd throw that head out."

The next day, she dons her pin-striped wedding suit and treats Jeanie to a movie. Afterward, she shops for a new spring wardrobe and splurges on a bottle of nail polish. The country girl has all but slipped away.

Baltimore, Maryland
March 21, 1945
Dear Mrs. Hammontree,

Since eight months have passed since "our" boys were reported missing, I thought it a good idea to write to all the families and see if by chance anyone has received some information—official or unofficial—regarding their whereabouts.

My husband, David Blake, is the co-pilot of the crew, and so far we have received no word of his welfare.

I suppose you know that Russell Becker and Wright McGee are prisoners. And with the war progressing so well, it shouldn't be long before they are liberated and can tell the story.

In the meantime, if you have some word of Gene, (who, by the way I met down in Tampa, and David and I used to go out to dinner with him and Joe, the bombardier, quite often) why, I would appreciate it if you will let me know. And I will do the same should I hear of David.

Sincerely,

Mrs. David Blake

Germany
April 1, 1945
Dear Velma,

I received a letter from you quite a few days ago, but we've been on the move and I didn't remember whether I answered your letter or not. I thought I'd just write while I was in the business.

You should see some of these places here in Germany. It's better than any picture show you ever saw in your life. We came to Germany through Belgium and Holland. There are lots of nice places between here and where we left France. I was in Metz and Nancy and lots of other smaller towns in France. I was also in Verdon. You may remember in history about the battle of Verdon in the last war. It's mostly forts and tunnels.

We aren't allowed to talk to the people in Germany, but I couldn't understand the lingo anyhow.

Have you heard from Bob lately? How is he doing over there? Is he still a machine gunner?

Write soon.

Love as ever,

Wayne

As are the ways in war, the Harrisonville paper runs a story that Friday on Dean Vansandt who was killed on Iwo Jima.

# HOME FRONT

# TWENTY-FIVE

**A**s much as she adores the city, Vee still spends weekends in Harrisonville. She pushes through the lack of sleep to attend church, but the music makes up for it. It is easy to swoon over Jimmy Davenport's bass voice. Norma sings in a quartet. Her in-laws are there, as is Mrs. Vansandt who suffers through the many condolences and well-wishes for the loss of her son.

At home, Vee decides to purge some of her belongings. She finds a few dresses that no longer appealed to her new fashion sense and asks her mother to pass them on. She reads through her original poetry and school essays with the thought of burning them. But her sheet music and books—she can not part with a single one.

One of the higher ups at P&W—a Mr. Paxton—informs Mr. Lane that one of the girls should have a professional reading taken of their brackets just to be sure the measurements are still within proper specifications. It will be necessary to send only one of the workers. As soon as Mr. Paxton leaves the room, all of the girls march to Tarzan's department, get the reading, and come back to their stations. Mr. Paxton is back and staring coldly at them.

"If we didn't put out more gears than any other department, we'd all be in big trouble," Vee mumbles to Kier. As it is, her next paycheck reflects a second raise.

A week into April, Doris plans a trip in her *Merry Oldsmobile* to Hartford, Connecticut to get her fur coat out of storage. "Molly, you and Vee should come along."

"But it's winter! What if we get stranded there?"

"No problem," Doris says. "We'll just work at the Hartford plant until it thaws out."

"We could fly instead of drive," Vee suggests.

Doris shakes her head. "Then we'd have to quit cheating on the hardness tester, cause we'd be flying with a Pratt & Whitney engine," she jokes.

April 12th, Loretta wakes Vee early. "Honey. I've got bad news," she says, sitting on the side of the bed. "President Roosevelt died this afternoon."

Vee struggles to comprehend Loretta's words. "What? No. I don't believe it."

"Yes, it's true. They say he had a stroke."

The women sit, stunned, on the bed and talk about what happens without Roosevelt to oversee the end to the horrible war that has overtaken their lives since Pearl Harbor was attacked.

"It makes me worry about Gene," Vee says, hugging her pillow. "Gene and Dad went all in for FDR. Outside of my relation, he and Bing Crosby were my favorite men."

Loretta cannot help but smile at the comment, then she looks thoughtfully at her boarder. "Truman will be sworn in, now. I hope he is up to the challenge."

Vee agrees. "But you know, Mrs. Roosevelt is still *First Lady* with me."

The P&W crew work soberly into the night. Everyone feels a little more responsibility at the news.

"Well, we'll finish the job, alright," Vee says to Kier. "I'm going to go buy a bond tomorrow in his honor. It wouldn't be much, but I think he'd like that."

Several of the girls agree to do the same.

***

The girls catch up with Sadie right before work one evening.

"You have to tell them your mother was sick."

"My mother? But it was my niece who was ill."

"I know that now," Vee says, but I accidentally told them it was your mother."

"What shall I say was wrong with her?"

"Oh, a bad case of heart trouble. Her first attack."

Sadie rolls her eyes and then practices the lie until she sounds sincere.

"Speaking of being ill," Vee says, "I have my tonsillectomy next Thursday. Don't know how long I'll need to recover."

Doris offers to lend her a book by Robert Service to read during her convalescence. The two have discovered a mutual love of poetry.

Thursday morning, Vee drinks a glass of orange juice—her last *meal* before surgery. Her mom meets her at Trinity Lutheran hospital for check-in.

"I feel like an infant," she says as Mildred helps her out of her clothes and into the hospital gown.

While she waits for surgery, she fills out a test in a magazine her mother brought. The test reaffirms what she already knows—she is typically a very happy person.

After the operation, Loretta shows up with roses, and Doris brings a card and three hankies from the girls at work. Vee pushes away the lunch tray, but by evening, she devours everything on the supper tray, even the toast. That proves to be a mistake.

The surgeon releases her the next day, and Loretta prepares a more suitable meal—bullion, mashed potatoes and gravy, Jello, and ice cream.

She feels her worst on Saturday. Loretta and the girls make her laugh which only irritates her throat. She bawls through her evening meal, but is determined to eat.

Though she still feels physically horrid on Sunday, the war news lifts everyone's spirits. Twenty-seven thousand allied prisoners of war in Germany—mostly airmen—have been rescued! If Gene is among them, the family should hear something soon.

Three days later, all of the Germans occupying northern Italy surrender, and Berlin has fallen. Hitler is officially reported dead.

> *Tampa, Florida*
> *May 5, 1945*
> *Dearest Vee,*
>
> *I hear you have taken care of your tonsils. Well, good. Maybe you wouldn't catch colds anymore. I'm glad Mom is going to be close to you for a while.*
>
> *The news is in our favor. They're keeping us in suspense about the surrender. Last Saturday, I was listening to the "Hit Parade" when they said that they had surrendered. I was so happy I just started yelling and crying. Of course, when they do surrender, we'll be happy, but that doesn't mean it's over as yet. Those Japs will give themselves up. They wouldn't get help from anybody, and they aren't going to fight us. That's my opinion. My brother says they're giving them trouble in the Philippines, but that a large number have been killed. They'd rather die than to surrender.*
>
> *Many boys are returning back from overseas. The war department gave orders for a rest camp at Drew Field. About eight train-loads of boys have already arrived here. Many more are coming and staying a short time and then they go to the Pacific.*
>
> *Well, Vee, I do hope you feel better. Tell Mom and Dad "hello" and also Harold, Bill and Hedrick.*
>
> *Love and luck,*
> *Carmen*

As part of her recovery, Vee stays the last half of the week in Harrisonville. She visits friends and writes a dozen letters. On Thursday, her in-laws pick her up for a stay. She is reminded of how much fun she can have with her husband. It is hard to separate her feelings for him from her love for his family.

Norma is late returning from Sunrise Breakfast on Sunday so, instead of church, the family drives to Bob's Aunt Effie's home for the afternoon. Cousin Ida Belle arrives looking very old fashioned and cute as a bug's ear. Bob's mother passes around two photos he sent home of pinup girls. Ida Belle requests one of the pictures to show her friends exactly what her cousin runs around with. Aunt Effie blushes deeply when someone suggests ordering her a duplicate.

"I wonder if it would make a good fire," Effie says.

"Indubitably," Vee says. "Through spontaneous combustion!"

The family attends Norma's baccalaureate. Vee swells with pride when her sister-in-law takes first in the citizenship award, and she wishes Norma could have the opportunity to go to college. Women have, after all, proven their capabilities and value during time of war.

Bob celebrates his twentieth birthday in the Pacific. One more year, and he will officially be a man—that is, if he makes it home. Surely, the Japanese will see the futility of their ways and join Germany in surrendering soon.

Her step-brother Hedrick enlists in the Navy. His training takes him to the Great Lakes before he is to ship out to California. One more brother to worry about. She missed seeing him on furlough while she was laid up in the hospital.

Vee returns to the city and to the news that Betty Faye has the mumps—the last thing Vee needs to hear after what she has been through. And their neighbor Mrs. Garrett is having a terrible time with her own tonsillectomy. Though Vee is on the mend, it takes some effort to regain her stamina at work.

"Would you like some tea?" Kier asks one night as she waves a tray of gauges under Vee's nose.

"Tea?"

"Why, yes. The T-16 gauge. Or maybe the T-163 gauge? I hear the T-67 gauge is quite tasty."

All the fun stops when Hudson tells the girls about her neighbor, a WWI veteran whose son is missing in action over Europe. The man's wife left him, so he tried to cut his own throat. He is not expected to survive.

Everyone grows silent and concentrates on whatever task assigned to them. Vee thinks of a man she knew who had lost his own son in war and then spent the rest of his life digging holes in his back yard. Everyone knew, and yet everyone passed the decimated yard as if each new mound of excavated dirt was just what was expected. A normal thing. She wonders if death would be cleaner.

As men from the European theater begin to return home, some of them bring War Brides with them. Bob's cousin Teddy is rumored to be in love with an Italian girl. Doris has met a French girl—the wife of a G.I. making port in Kansas City. She has been in the States a month, and Doris can barely understand her English.

"She's very dark, pretty, and graceful," Doris says. "I'll arrange a lunch so you girls can meet her."

"That sounds lovely," everyone agrees. "We were allies in Europe. We'll be allies here."

Mary Kay comes down with the mumps, but only on one side.

# TWENTY-SIX

**M**ay warms into a beautiful spring inspiring the city to open its windows wide. Vee wakes to another Sunday service, this time from a pipe organ at a nearby Baptist church. She listens to the piercing high notes, the rumbling bass notes, and the mass of voices wailing out a sacred noise.

The extended Long family invites her on a picnic at Swope park, and it seems the entire city has come to the same decision. Everywhere they go, the twins draw extra attention from passersby. One stranger stops to admire them and asks, "Which of you is which?"

Mary Kay raises her hand and says, "I'm which."

The girls have inherited their mother's sarcasm.

Vee and Jeanie wander off to ride the miniature train and bike the paths. The girls watch longingly as couples walk hand in hand or sit together in deep conversation on the grass. They talk about the fun Jeanie has out with her girlfriends on Saturday night—one more thing Vee can not participate in.

"Wish I could have gone with you. I often hate me for the things I don't do."

She grumbles at how night shift wreaks havoc on her leisure time and how much the girls dislike their supervisor. "I'd slave for Millie if I could work in her department. She's hard, and she can really dish it out. But unlike Lane, she can take it, too!"

That evening, Vee writes to everyone in her world—her mom and mother-in-law, Bob, Carmen, Wayne, Mrs. Corn, and Betty whom she has taken to calling *Professor* Corn. She writes a letter to Gene, but merely folds it away in a drawer.

***

The lights go out for two hours that night at work. Everyone stumbles their way into the lunch room and finds places to sit in the dark. The conversations wander over a hundred random topics.

"They're asking eighty-five cents a dozen!" Harry exclaims. "And if you just want one orange, it's a dern seven and a half cents."

"I can't afford them anyway," Molly says. "Someone swiped my billfold on the elevator. I had fourteen bucks in there!"

Kier jumps in. "My postman was struck by lightning last week. Severely burned."

"Oh no! I hope he recovers."

"Me, too. I miss him. I always ask him if he has letters for me today. He says *lots of them. Postage due, of course.*"

"So, what do you make of the new cafeteria-styled restaurants? Lanes, runways, and stalls, as if we were cattle."

"Yeah, Mary and I walk down the aisle and try to figure out how to get to the tables."

"Disgusting," Mary says. "A damn trap, that's all it is."

Sadie speaks quietly. "Did you hear about the newborn they found in a trash can? Gosh, I hope it's going to be alright. Who would do that?"

In the dark, Millie leans into Sadie's space. "And how would you explain a baby to Jack when he's been gone for two years?"

Thankful that no one can see, a number of women on the line blush at the accusation, but Sadie's eyes narrow as she squares her shoulders. "Well, I wouldn't throw it away!"

In the silence that falls, Millie changes the subject to living in Ravenwood north of the river. It sounds like a beautiful subdivision.

"I would love to see Loretta's uncle's place," Vee says. "Built before the Civil War. Bullet holes in the door. Five fireplaces. The walls are a foot and half thick! It was built by Negro slaves out of handmade bricks." The subject of slavery makes her uncomfortable, so she adds, "When the war was over, Tom bought all of his slaves some land and built them log houses." She admires Tom for what she sees as benevolence, though she understands little about the hardships of a sharecropper's life.

"My dad's an inventor," Hudson says. "Our family has always been hard to wake up, so when I was a kid, he set up four alarm clocks to go off five minutes apart. I don't remember how, but he connected the last one to a lamp and a radio! By the time we were all awake, so was everyone else on the block!"

The lights come back on. The girls start rushing around and asking if their hair is a mess. Millie looks at Lane sitting beside her and asks, "Is my lipstick on straight?" He simply scowls at their antics.

Even with the two-hour break, it's a hard night's work. Vee sleeps most of the next day. When her alarm sounds, she finds a note from Loretta saying they have gone to the cemetery for Decoration Day, and they will be sure to lay flowers on her Uncle Raymond's grave. So many kindnesses, and yet, the reminder of so many war dead sparks nightmares over the next few days of Gene and her father, even though her father has never been to war.

With the focus of the war shifting toward the Pacific, production at the plant slows a bit. Even Lane quits pushing them as hard. In June, enough people leave the plant that Lane needs to pick up slack on one of the production lines. Vee smiles every time she sees the little frown line on his forehead.

On a Wednesday afternoon, Vee shops on Prospect Avenue. She pauses at the window of *Ye Old Book Shop* and, for curiosity's sake, steps in. The interior of the shop is floor-to-ceiling books, most fraying at the bindings and covered in various amounts of dust.

"Can I help you?"

She sees an elderly man in faded clothes a size too big for his frame.

"I'm looking for books on poetry."

His eyes come alive. "Any one in particular?"

"No. I love all poetry. Do you have anything to recommend?"

The man pulls a book from behind the counter. "A Hundred and One Famous Poets!" He holds the ancient tome up for her to see. "This is my personal copy."

Vee thinks he must have the original printing.

"I love poetry," he continues. "I read one out of this book every single night."

"Do you live nearby?"

He points at a set of stairs leading to the second-floor apartment. "Upstairs. Name's Pop. Here, let me show you around." He wanders off into the stacks.

The store reminds Vee of an ancient library, neglected by all but the man who cares for it. He escorts her through the various sections and points out his recommendations. When they reach the cookbooks, he pulls a tattered one off the shelf and opens it to a much-fondled page.

"Here's a recipe for *Cheap Layer Cake*. Break up two pounds of butter. Two pounds! Ha! Nothing cheap about that these days. Why, you'd be hard pressed to get a half a pound even with ration stamps."

Vee purchases two books and assures Pop that she will return often.

*Tampa, Florida*
*June 20, 1945*
*Dearest Vee,*

    *Long time no hear from. Is anything wrong? Are you still working? I received a letter from Mom this week.*

    *You never tell me anything about Bob. I guess he's overseas, right? All the boys will soon be back. Just as soon as we wipe out the dirty Japs. I don't believe they have a strong resistance. They'll give up sooner or later. Brother is having a hot time out in the Philippines. I hope everything turns out alright with him.*

    *It seems as if all my girl friends are getting married but me. I'm not worried, though, as I'm still young and have a lot of time ahead of me. After all, marriage is not a play thing. You have to really think it over before you do get married.*

    *I was looking at the calendar, and I see the 29th will be Gene's birthday. I hope he shows up for a big celebration. How wonderful it will be.*

    *Love and Luck,*
    *Carmen*

On June 21, Vee skips sleep so she and the night shift girls can walk to Union Station. The enormous crowds stretch from the station all the way up the grassy mall toward the Liberty Memorial. The P&W crew work their way to the west side of the mall and claim their seats on the lawn with a good view of Pershing Road.

"Why are we here again?" Kier asks.

"Soldiers and sailors," Boone says to her, pointing to the regiments as they high-step their way past in perfect formation.

"It's not like we'll get to meet any of them." Vee can feel the sun bearing down on the back of her neck and wonders what kind of burn she will suffer over the next few days.

"Look! It's General Eisenhower!"

The crowd that had been cheering continuously for the boys in uniform jumps to its feet and roars at the sight of the man they believe saved them all from Hitler's fascism. It is a beautiful day. A beautiful parade. Hope for a resolution in the Pacific permeates the air.

At three in the afternoon, the girls try to enter the station, but the crowds prevent them from getting anywhere near a water fountain, so they hike all the way to 10th Street before finding a restaurant with room enough.

"Wasn't that just swell?" Vee says when they are seated. "Just think, we'll have another one when the Japanese finally surrender."

Discussion turns to disturbing reports about New Caledonians torturing captured Japanese soldiers and burning them alive. The Americans are against the practice, but can do little to stop it. When the girls order chow mein, Vee turns up her nose, using the excuse that she does not care for Asian food.

"It looks even worse than what I tasted in California." She drinks water and wishes for a more benign subject around the dinner table.

At the plant, Vee manages to nap in the locker room and still get out a decent night's work. She spends her afternoons riding and swimming with friends, and her evenings trying to sleep to the sounds of the Hit Parade, the opera, or the philharmonic.

"Oh, my fiery sunburn," she complains one evening. "Even the tops of my feet and the ends of my big toes!"

"We'll start calling you Lobster Legs," Loretta says.

Vee laughs and then gives Loretta a smirking grin. "I've heard it's a sin to jest on Sunday."

"And why do you suppose that is?"

"Maybe they just have no sense of humor. I've decided that a lot of people believe in the Bible more than they believe in God. To me, that's silly."

Loretta smiles.

# TWENTY-SEVEN

**Work. Sleep. Music. Letters. Poetry. Picnics. Life on repeat.**
June melts into July, making it harder for Vee to sleep during the hot afternoons that bring most of the city out of doors. She manages her routine as best she can.

Bob writes of a bombing run over one of the islands they were hoping to capture. When the plane returned to base, he stood up off of his parachute and saw that a bullet had gone clean through it from side to side. He was grateful not only to be alive, but that he had not had to jump with his chute full of holes.

It is one year to the day that Gene had been declared missing when Vee hears the rumor. On the way home from work, a coworker says Clifton Long has heard that a member of Gene's crew bailed out of the plane when it was hit, and shortly after that, the plane exploded. It is devastating news. Vee holds herself together enough to buy a bus ticket to Harrisonville.

When she confronts her step-mom, Mildred laughs. "Honey, you didn't need to come all the way down here. I wrote you a letter that should arrive tomorrow."

Vee's mouth drops open, and her eyes fill with tears. "Tomorrow? Or next week? Or a month from now? What's the difference? I'm only his sister!" For the first time in her life, Vee is angry at her step-mom—an anger that she cannot control. "How long have you known?"

Mildred goes to the table and offers Vee two letters. The first is dated three weeks prior.

> *War Department*
> *28 June 1945*
> *Dear Mr. Hammontree:*
>
> *I am writing to you concerning your son, Second Lieutenant Eugene L. Hammontree who has been reported missing in action since 18 July 1944 over Germany.*
>
> *The anxiety you have suffered since receiving the announcement is most understandable and I realize your desire to learn the circumstances attending his disappearance. A report has now been received in the War Department containing information obtained from Technical Sergeant Wright W. McGee who was a member of your son's crew and who has been evacuated to the United States. This report states that your son's crew departed from their base on their final mission at 7:30 a.m., to the target area which was to be an airdrome at Memmingen, Germany. The aircraft sustained damage by enemy fighter planes approximately ten miles from Kempten, Germany, and shells exploding within the plane caused it to ignite. Sergeant McGee left the engineer's compartment through the bomb bay and entered the radio room which had been vacated by Technical Sergeant Mearl E. Daufeldt, the radioman. He then proceeded to the waist of the plane where he planned to bail out. Sergeant McGee states that Staff Sergeant Charles W. Nichols and Staff Sergeant Robert N. Giard, the waist gunners, had already bailed out. In the waist of the plane he discovered Staff Sergeant Russell E. Becker unconscious, due to wounds and lack of oxygen. Sergeant McGee checked Sergeant Becker's parachute, found it in order, then assisted him through the waist door of the plane. He then bailed out himself and, upon looking back at the plane, after his parachute had opened, he observed that it appeared to explode in the air.*

*Sergeant McGee landed and was immediately taken into custody by German farmers and removed to a farm house. He was picked up by an ambulance about six hours later and transported to a hospital located at Kempten, Germany. Sergeant Becker and Sergeant McGee remained at the hospital in Kempten from 18 July to 1 August 1944. Neither of these men was able to obtain any information regarding the remainder of the crew during that time. They were then transferred, by hospital train, to Frankfurt, Germany. Sergeant Becker remained there and Sergeant McGee was taken on the Obermasfeldt Prisoner of War Hospital where he remained until 15 September 1944. He was then transferred to Stalag Luft #4 until 31 January 1945; then to Stalag Luft #1, where he remained until liberated by the Russians on 1 May 1945. During these various moves, Sergeant McGee failed to obtain any information regarding his crew. I can well understand your distress occasioned by the absence of any further information regarding your son's whereabouts; however, you have my assurance that you will be promptly informed of any additional details which may become available regarding Lieutenant Hammontree.*

*You have my sincere sympathy during this long and trying period of uncertainty.*

*Sincerely yours,*

*J. A. Ulio*

*Major General*

*The Adjutant General of the Army*


*Amarillo, Texas*

*July 9, 1945*

*Dear Mr. and Mrs. Hammontree,*

*Wright is home, and we are all very happy. Surely wish everyone could be as happy as we are. I was so in hopes you would receive good news concerning Eugene.*

*Wright doesn't know very much to tell you as he was badly injured when he bailed out. The plane was on fire, and he is pretty sure it blew up after he bailed out. At least, he has been told it did. As far as he knows, the officers and tail gunner didn't get out of the plane. Wright was the fifth one to bail out.*

*Surely wish we could tell you something which would ease your broken hearts. We will be glad to hear from you any time you care to write.*

*Sincerely,*

*Wright and Julie McGee*

Vee looks questioningly at her mom. "We still don't know?"

Mildred reaches for her daughter's shoulders and squeezes them tightly. "Honey, that's why I hadn't told you yet. Nothing is certain."

***

It is cruel, not knowing. Every-day joys are tainted by the idea that she should be grieving for Gene. Yet, if it is true that he died when the plane was first hit, there is small comfort in the fact that he did not starve in a prison camp or was not tortured to death on some God-forsaken island in the Pacific. Still, she cannot bring herself to mourn. Not yet.

The War Department sends another letter—a matter of paperwork to clean up their own loose ends.

*The Adjutant General's Office*

*19 July 1945*

*Dear Mr. Hammontree:*

*Since your son was reported missing in action 18 July 1944, the War Department has entertained the hope that he survived and that information would be revealed dispelling the uncertainty surrounding his absence. However, as in many cases, the conditions of warfare deny us such information.*

*Full consideration has recently been given to all available information bearing on the absence of your son, including all records, reports and circumstances. In view of the fact that twelve months have now expired without the receipt of evidence to support a continued presumption of survival, the War Department must terminate such absence by a presumptive finding of death. Accordingly, an official finding of death has been recorded under the provisions of Public Law 490, 77th Congress, approved March 7, 1942, as amended.*

*The finding does not establish an actual or probable date of death; however, as required by law, it includes a presumptive date of death for the termination of pay and allowances, settlement of accounts and payment of death gratuities. In the case of your son, this date has been set as 19 July 1945.*

*I regret the necessity for this message but trust that the ending of a long period of uncertainty may give at least some small measure of consolation. I hope you may find sustaining comfort in the thought that the uncertainty with which war has surrounded the*

*absence of your son has enhanced the honor of his service to his country and of his sacrifice.*
*Sincerely yours,*
*Edward F. Witsell*
*Major General*
*Acting The Adjutant General of the Army*

On the bus back to the city, Vee wavers between hope and the resolution that Gene is gone. She strikes up a conversation with a woman beside her and prattles on about his antics over the years.

"He was a good guy—the best! You can tell the world that!"

Loretta welcomes her with a hug and a patient ear. She fixes a lovely evening meal and then sends her boarder to bed. When the time comes for Vee to dress for work, Loretta opens the bedroom door and stares a while at the young woman who has been through so much turmoil in a single year. She quietly steps to the bedside and makes sure the alarm is turned off, then she closes the door and goes to bed.

# HOME FRONT

# TWENTY-EIGHT

*Sedalia Army Air Field*
*30 July 1945*
*My dear Mr. Hammontree,*

*I regret very much the necessity of writing to you, but I am anxious to add what words of comfort I can at this time.*

*Few words of mine can express the sorrow we all feel in the loss of any personnel, whether attached to our own respective units, or as in this case, one serving in another unit. In writing this letter, it is my privilege to extend to you the sympathy and regrets of General H. H. Arnold, AAF, as well as those of all personnel represented in this branch of the Armed Services.*

*I hope you will find some consolation in the fact that your son died for those same things which he believed — even as it is possible that many more of us shall make the supreme sacrifice for those same ideals. Far better is it to have lived and died in a steadfast defense of ideals than to be slaves of others who do our thinking for us. So to this end, we are all pledged — that none of our men shall die in vain, but shall become enshrined in our hearts that we may make their ideals and dreams come true for those of coming generations.*

*May I commend you to the One Father of all mercies whose love and compassion may heal your bitterest sorrow and dry your deepest tear, in the sure and certain knowledge and His strength and comfort can help you in these unhappy days.*

*God richly bless you in this your sacrifice for country, home, and freedom.*

*Most sincerely,*

*Willis M. Lewis*

*Chaplain (Maj) USA*

Vee finds refuge in the usual places—work, play, books, music, shopping—but stories that might not have impressed her in the past begin to shape how she views her place in the world. Merle Oberon's portrayal of George Sand, Frederick Chopin's lover—a woman who took on a man's name and clothing, and dared to make her way in a man's world—inspires Vee's own strong will. She thinks Sand right about a lot of things. If nothing else, Vee cannot get Chopin's *Polonaise* out of her head the entire night at work.

Lane informs the girls that, due to slowed production, the department needs thinning, and some of them are assigned new positions. Vee reports to Millie the next night. She is elated.

"Poor Hudson. She'll have to work with Mitch in 761. Too bad they hate each other now."

"Could be worse," Vee says. "You should have heard what these two women on the bus were talking about today. I swear. One of them said she liked a guy named Frank, but Frank was using her money to buy another girl drinks. She hopes she's pregnant so Frank will marry her."

Sadie shivers from head to toe. "That's the height of ignorance. If she's lucky, Frank will take a powder."

"If she's lucky. Gee. I wonder what life would be like if we didn't need a man at all."

The girls think it over and come to the same conclusion. "Awful!" they yell in unison.

"Yeah," Kier says. "Can't live with 'em, and...you know the rest."

Vee attempts to sleep the next morning, but her mind races with thoughts of people and life and death, and about Gene. He was one of the good guys, she reminds herself. Her brother's life had held so much potential, so much he could have shared with the world. But she also realizes that, despite losing a part of herself in him, she now has a part of his life to live along with her own. The idea makes her homesick.

A tenant downstairs begins to play Polonaise. Vee empties her mind and lets the music carry her into a deep and restful sleep.

*Tampa, Florida*

*August 4, 1945*

*Dearest Vee,*

*I still have hopes even though they seem very dark. I guess I never was lucky in my life, everything turned against me all the time. And now, when I started to see great happiness ahead, this had to happen. I'll always carry Gene in my heart.*

*All my girlfriends try to get me to go out with other boys, but I can't. I don't enjoy myself. I can't help it. I envy the happiness of others and hate to see them happy. I know I'm selfish, but I can't help feeling this way.*

*Vee, do you know if his friend Joe bailed out or not? The boys that did bail out don't tell much. I'd like for them to write to me. Every time I see a boy with the arm patch from the 15th Air Force, I run and ask them all the information I can get from them. They're not much help, but it relieves my mind a little.*

*We had open field here Wednesday. I went with five other girls. Everything I saw reminded me of Gene, and I couldn't help but cry all through the special ceremony. I saw all the equipment the navigators use. He really was smart to be able to use all those instruments.*

*All my love always,*

*Carmen*

*The Secretary of War*
*August 4, 1945*
*My dear Mr. Hammontree:*

*At the request of the President, I write to inform you that the Purple Heart has been awarded posthumously to your son, Second Lieutenant Eugene L. Hammontree, Air Corps, who sacrificed his life in defense of his country.*

*Little that we can do or say will console you for the death of your loved one. We profoundly appreciate the greatness of your loss, for in a very real sense the loss suffered by any of us in this battle for our country is a loss shared by all of us. When the medal, which you will shortly receive, reaches you, I want you to know that with it goes my sincerest sympathy, and the hope that time and the victory of our cause will finally lighten the burden of your grief.*

*Sincerely yours,*
*Henry L. Stimson*

***

In spite of her loss—or maybe because of it—Vee searches out joy in small things. In the heat of August, she and Loretta throw wash water at each other, often ending up as wet as the clothes they are cleaning. When Loretta nearly catches her hand in the wringer one afternoon, Vee formulates a mystery novel in her mind. "*The Case of the Wrung Hand.*"

"I always wanted to write one called *The Case of the Violin.*"

Their jokes send Vee to Pop's bookstore in search of a good read, and on to Jenkins Music where she purchases a lovely hand-painted music box for her mom. It plays *Blue Danube* and *Tales from the Vienna Woods.* To her delight, she spots a book of Chopin's piano pieces and the sheet music for *Clair de Lune.* As she steps to the counter to pay, a young blonde girl who works at the store sits at one of the pianos on the showroom floor and begins to play Gershwin's *Rhapsody in Blue.* Everyone gathers around to listen.

Vee steps back into the summer heat and finds herself wishing for an early snowfall. Not that she is ungrateful for summer, but she needs a new direction for her life. And there is something purifying about a pristine first snow.

War imposes its ugly head once more, but Vee refuses to dwell on it. Even after the unrelenting jabber at work, she simply writes, "That atomic bomb is really something. The talk of the Earth." But with the bomb comes the expectation that Japan will surrender soon. Everyone holds their breath while waiting for the news.

"Dear Diary, Slept all day and woke up listening to hear of Jap surrender. But no. They have to be stubborn."

The end of the war means something else—Bob's return home. Not only does Vee question her commitment to him, but she knows he intends to return to his father's farm. She wonders if she can give up the city she has grown to love.

The Pratt & Whitney crew decides to each have their pictures taken and to trade them. They know their jobs will not last much longer. But if not P&W, then where? It will be difficult for any of them to trade their coveted freedom for the security as a housewife.

On August 12th, the country receives a false report of a Japanese surrender. The joke at work is "Hirohito has atomic ache."

On August 14th, at 2:30 in the morning, Sadie and Vee call the night desk at the Kansas City Star. "There is nothing official," is the response. So they play keep-away in the corridor for a while, and then go back to work.

On August 14th, at 6:00 in the evening, Loretta wakes Vee to the news. Japan has surrendered unconditionally. Within minutes, the family hears the noise as people crowd into the streets. It sounds like New Year's Eve and Christmas all in one. Drivers honk their horns, and residents throw water out of windows. People stand in the streets and cheer. The twins ask their mother if they can do something *treacherous*.

"Peace at last for China, and after nine years," Vee says. "Maybe Dude and Wayne will be home soon." She realizes too late that she has forgotten to mention Bob. Of course, she wants him home safe.

Vee had been motherless, a child of The Depression, a country girl. She had played the role of girlfriend, fiancée, wife. She learned how better to relate as a sister and a friend. She has grown into an aesthete—

appreciating art, music, literature—and learned to thrive on urban energy. She has lived and played as an independent working woman. Now, she is jobless, grieving her brother, and still married to a man she barely knows.

When Loretta's family takes a much-needed vacation, they drop Vee in Harrisonville so she can spend time with family and reconnect with her roots. It is far less comforting than she hopes. Thoughtful conversation with her mom on the porch cannot not sustain her through the many drawn-out, uninteresting stories her grandmother Ora comes to share. And when Vee wakes early, she realizes her mistake during the after-breakfast stories Ora takes the unnecessary trouble to tell. To escape, Vee reads stories on the backs of cereal boxes, picks chickens, and helps—or hinders—cousin Eddie to chore.

"Do you belong to a church?" her grandmother asks over lunch.

"Yes, but don't feel sorry for me. It was my own fault."

Ora glowers at her over a set of wire-rim spectacles.

While much of the world celebrates peace, Vee fights difficult memories of both her brother's passing and her failing marriage. She hides as much as she can from her in-laws, still spending pleasant nights in their company, but she becomes increasingly disillusioned about the chances of her and Bob building a loving relationship. She no longer sees herself as a farm wife.

On a day trip with Norma into the city, Vee admits, "The more I see of the country, the more I hate it." She anxiously awaits the end of Loretta and Ken's vacation so she can return to what she now considers *home*.

From one of the many books she buries herself in, Vee notes in her diary a portion of a quote attributed to Sir Isaac Newton.

*"I don't know what I may seem to the world, but as to myself, I seem to have been only like a boy playing on the sea-shore...whilst the great ocean of truth lay all undiscovered before me."*

Wave after wave of truth begins to erode the sand beneath her feet. After much deliberation, she determines that her happiness depends on finding new work in the city, and on securing her own livelihood so that she will be beholden to no man.

# TWENTY-NINE

**Vee returns to the city at the end of August.** "Professor" Corn writes about the experience of starting college—another thing Vee wants to envy Betty for.

After turning in her badge and locker key to Pratt & Whitney, she rides streetcars in search of work that may replace her lost income but also give her a sense of purpose. After spotting an ad for Hall's, she tries her hand at verse but comes to the conclusion that the company is full of particular people—people she does not *particularly* care for.

When the Kansas City Public Library advertises for help, Vee cannot contain her enthusiasm.

"Wouldn't that be too too wonderful?" she asks Jeanie.

Jeanie acts less enthralled, but applies for a position as well. "By the looks of their staff, they only hire old maids. We probably don't stand a chance."

"You know the difference between a bachelor girl and an old maid, don't you? A bachelor girl has never been married, and an old maid has never been married or *anything*!"

While the days pass without a job offer, Vee sews, writes letters, listens to the radio, and sees the occasional movie.

Her dad receives Gene's purple heart medal and the paperwork to start processing his life insurance payout—heartbreak overpowering the pride of his service. On one visit, Vee gives her mom the music box. It is hard to know if Mildred likes it, but Vee suspects that Mom likes things more than she lets on.

*Tampa, Florida*
*September 20, 1945*
*Dearest Vee,*

> *Please forgive me for not writing sooner. Dee got married, and I've been awfully busy. I was one of her maids. We were suppose to have ushers, but they were restricted to camp because of the hurricane. We really had some excitement around here, but thank God it didn't do much damage.*
>
> *Vee, please don't think that I don't want to continue our writing to one another, because I do. I have learned to love you and the rest of the family like I do my own, even though I haven't had the honor of meeting you in person. Next summer, I have high hopes in meeting and staying with you for a short time.*
>
> *Please tell Mom to write me. I have written to her, and she hasn't answered as yet.*
> *Love Always,*
> *Carmen*

Pratt & Whitney mails her last paycheck, so Vee calls the library to see if any decision has been made. When they have nothing definite to tell her, she takes a job in the arts and crafts division at Hall's with the hopes that she will not be there long. Four days later, the library offers her a position.

To celebrate, Vee purchases two new pieces of sheet music—*Look for the Silver Lining* and *Theme from Warsaw Concerto*. Though the latter is beyond her skill, she asks the young blonde at Jenkins to play the piece on the showroom floor. Again, everyone in the store stops to listen to the impromptu concert.

On her first day home from the library, she can hardly contain her excitement. "I love all the people!" she tells Loretta. "Jane Brinton must have introduced me to twenty people, all of them nice as pie. They treat me like a human there. You know, I got the job because I told them how much I love to read."

Her enthusiasm for the library grows with every shift. The patrons warm to her personality, and her coworkers quickly draw her into their social circles. Jane had been a writer, but complains that it is unprofitable. She had once seen Irene Dunne and Bing Crosby at the Kentucky Derby. Grace has such a smiling way of telling things that Vee is laughing before she is finished. Helen wants to be a nun. Though work in general instilled in Vee a sense of independence, the library inspires her to seek gratification in building a career.

Kier, from P&W, stays in touch, sharing the latest gossip on the old crew. Sadie is trying to make another go of it with Jack. Bonnie works for Bell Telephone. Boone is working for an insurance company and dating a guy who sells soap.

As September rushes into October, Gene is never far away in Vee's thoughts. One of her coworkers compliments her on her positive attitude toward life, commenting that she must be related to Pollyanna. Vee believes Gene must have had something to do with that, as he was always happy. He lived each day as though it might be his last, but little did he know how soon that last day would come.

The insurance company continues to work through the business of death benefits while the government sends notice that Gene's bonds would now need to be probated to the next of kin. More and more, Vee finds comfort in the written word. She recalls a poem by Mary Carolyn Davies and notes it in her diary.

*Dim your bright hills this year, October,*
*Deprive them of the sumac's flaming red;*
*Drape the valley with wistful smoke wreaths,*
*Someone we loved is dead.*

*Temper your lavish gold this year, October,*
*Render the landscape brown and sere;*
*We will not ask you to do this always,*
*Only . . . . this year.*

On November 11th—Armistice Day—the Pleasant Ridge Baptist Church holds a memorial for Gene. The sanctuary is crowded with family and friends, and overflowing with beautiful flowers. As the pastor talks of heroism and sacrifice and a place for God's chosen, Vee's mind centers on a line from Shakespeare's *Coriolanus*. "I do love my country's good with a respect more tender, more holy, more profound, than mine own life." She needs to find her comfort in the fact that Gene believe in that good—in the cause that sent him beyond anyone's reach now.

Jeanie's family receives word that Dude will be home by Christmas. No word when Bob or Wayne will be discharged.

Vee continues to spend time with her best friend, but she finds the company of the women at the library increasingly more intellectually stimulating. One afternoon, she meets with Jane and her mother for lunch. Mrs. Brinton is just as she pictured her—small and gray and charming. A perfect lady. Vee is reminded of her aunts, the Kohntopp women. Most had been well-schooled in their day, and all seem self-assured. Gleaning what she can from her biological mother's family, Vee imagines that Jane's mother and her own possess that same quiet surety—even-tempered and calm with a measure of unassuming class.

In early December, the library receives six hundred visitors a day, most asking for the bindery. As Christmas approaches, many seek the repair or embellishment of precious family books. It is the seventy-second anniversary of the library's founding, and though the institution has already changed locations once, it has outgrown the 9th and Locust location. The institution is a hub of human interaction.

An optimistic peace combined with storefront decorations and the occasional light snow puts shoppers in the mood to search out the perfect Christmas gifts for family and friends. Vee takes advantage of every opportunity to window shop before and after work. For Harold Dean, Bill, and Hedrick, she buys matching identification bracelets and has each brother's name engraved into them. She purchases a lovely piece of delicate silk and cuts it into strips, hemming the edges to make scarves for a number of her women friends. To her delight, the stores offer a nice selection of hosiery—something that had been in rare supply during the war. Vee buys herself two pair.

When traffic at the library slows, she picks an interesting book from a shelf and hides just out of sight to sneak a few minutes of coveted reading time. Robert, the page at the reference desk, can be found the next aisle over. The two of them frequently share opinions and recommendations, and cover for each other when Jane comes looking. In all other respects, Vee is a model librarian. Her ever-increasing knowledge of poetry and literature endear her to the patrons who often seek her out.

As festive as the city looks in its seasonal trimmings, Vee resists the holiday cheer. The thought that her husband will return home soon raises a subtle panic in her chest. She feels sure that Bob will not make an effort to find work in the city, and she cannot bear the idea of living on a farm. It is a cruel twist of fate that the war inspired so many women to marry in haste and then recruited them into the workforce, giving them a taste of autonomy and power. All around her, she watches capable and successful women fall back into subservient roles as their men return from war. But her coworkers at the library show Vee the possibilities of living an independent life. The unmarried librarians are often the brunt of jokes—referred to as *old maids or spinsters*. Once upon a time, Vee felt sorry for any woman in that position. Now, she refuses to pity Jane who lives a deliberate life opposed to social pressure and expectation. Oh, to be her.

Vee buys presents for everyone on her list, but each dinner, each visit with family is tempered by the thought that soon she will have to make a decision about her marriage. In her heart, she is already divorced. The bigger question is where and how to live. Loretta and Ken have been so generous to take her in, but she cannot impose on their generosity much longer. Perhaps one of her coworkers needs a roommate. After the holidays, she will search out rentals.

On the last day of 1945, Vee works her shift at the library. In the morning, she takes a call from a woman demanding the address that they should have on file for a Mr. Thayer.

"I will need permission to give out an address."

"But I'm a taxpaying citizen!" the woman bellows. "I want the address of that skunk!"

Vee writes down her name and number and, after looking up the man's information, calls him for permission to pass it on. When someone answers the phone, she asks, "Is Mr. Thayer there?"

"No, he's not." The woman's voice is rather curt.

"Do you know when he might return?"

"Hell, I don't know, lady. Maybe you want him to come back, but I never want to see him again!"

Vee tosses the first woman's number into the trash.

At noon, Loretta brings the twins by so the four of them can lunch together. After work, Vee and Jane celebrate the New Year by having supper at the California Steak House and then seeing *The Bells of St. Mary's* with "that Crosby man" and Ingred Bergman. Both agree it is a marvelous film.

When the women step out of the theater, they join the mob at 12th and Baltimore. Nearly everyone appears drunk—strangers kissing strangers, people lighting fires up and down the streets. They throw confetti everywhere. It feels like VJ Day all over again.

# THIRTY

The second of January, Vee returns to work, though she spends most of her day staying out of Miss Johnson's way. The mood lightens when someone leaves a four-pound box of Stover's chocolates at the front desk. John vows to destroy all evidence. Still, Vee has a rather dull day as all the "crazies" had been in before the new year.

On her way home, she stops to buy a pair of black pumps for winter and a pair of brown sandals for summer. Along with the shoes, she purchases a 1946 diary. When she reaches the apartment on Brooklyn Avenue, Loretta is pulling five aluminum packages out of the oven.

"I thought we'd try these new-fangled frozen dinners. Each package is a meal in itself! Chicken. Green beans. Mashed potatoes." Steam rises up from each tray as Loretta peels back the foil tops.

"I swear," Vee says shaking her head. "Someday we'll live on vitamin pills."

"What about our stomachs?"

"Oh, they'll gradually shrink in size."

Loretta looks down at her own and prayerfully says, "Oh hasten the day!"

The family attends Wayne's birthday dinner at Mom and Pop Long's house on Sunday. All morning, Clifton whines about his hunger. Betty Jo decides to test his patience by setting a roaster pan on the table. She places a butcher knife and ladle to one side, and a meat fork on the other. At the point of the knife, she places a quart jar of water. In the roaster, she lays a sprig of lettuce and half an onion.

"What is this?" Clif asks when she brings him in. "No gravy?"

The actual meal beats anything coming out of a frozen tray. After they eat, Vee and her friends drive to Swope Park. At the zoo, they wander through the animal houses, eat peanuts, buy balloons. In the chimpanzee house, Jeanie leans toward one of the cages and says, "Well, Dale! I thought you were in California!"

Vee loves the city, her job, her friends, Loretta's family. Her and Bob's relationship has improved through their letters, but she wanders if it is enough to keep them together. Even so, her heart falls when Loretta informs her that two of Bob's letters have been returned, unopened.

"No forwarding address," Loretta says with a sympathetic frown.

"No." Vee tries to put on a smile before sitting down to dinner.

"We're having spare ribs," Mary Kay informs her. "I wonder."

"What?"

"How many ribs does a pig have, counting his spare ones?"

The twins are a bright spot in Vee's life. They help to lighten her otherwise frustrated evenings when the mailbox fails to produce what she desires most.

"What am I to do?" she ponders. "Go mad!"

On January 19th, Loretta phones Vee at work. Bob is back in the States. Her feelings are a jumble of happiness, relief, and an underlying dread. As requested, she stops off after work and buys Bob some new "civies" to replace his uniforms.

She buses to Harrisonville and meets most of the family at Ella's in town. Her Aunt Anna brakes the news that cousin Sophia Barbara has passed from rheumatic fever. Vee finds it impossible to grasp the sorrow of losing one so young and talented, and on the cusp of a Hollywood career.

It is a somber ride out to her in-laws where the family is celebrating the return of their war hero. Bob certainly looks the part—a six-foot, handsome man in his Army Air Corp attire. He sweeps his wife into his arms and kisses her unabashedly in front of everyone.

"I brought your clothes," she says, pulling away and lowering her head to hide the flush in her cheeks.

The last time Vee saw her husband was the day she left California. The day she had determined that their relationship was dead. Fatefully, it was also the day her brother died. So much heartbreak. Both friends and family had admonished her to try again. And she did. In the following months, Vee let her husband back into her heart. His letters were sweet, and his gifts thoughtful. But as he stands beside her now, she feels the darker side of him honed by the war. She thinks back to the photo he sent, his eyes betraying his smile.

Over the next few days, the two of them shuffle between the city Vee loves and the country where both of them grew up. The striking contrast between the two serves to frustrate her even more. She takes a few days off to accommodate her husband's return and to show him the possibilities Kansas City has to offer—culture, jobs, entertainment—but Bob is set on helping his dad with the farm. More than once, she tries to excuse herself from time at his folks.

Vee insists on keeping her job at the library, so Bob moves into 3030 Brooklyn Avenue. When the two are not at the movies or out with friends, they help Loretta with household chores. Most of the time, Bob taunts his wife about her growing independence.

Vee arrives at work on Monday to find Jane in a chipper mood.

"William wants me to go with him to California on vacation."

"Why not?" she asks. "He's silly about you."

"I'm just not sure what to do," Jane says, and before she can finish her thought, Glenda bursts in.

"Hello, you two! Excited to see me?" She winks at Vee and rounds the circulation desk. "Last day before I become a Mrs."

"We're so happy for you," Jane says.

Vee nods. "Johnny is such a swell guy. You better treat him right."

"Treat him right? What about poor little ole me?"

Jane pulls a gift from under the counter. "We got you this."

Glenda tears into the package and pulls out a beautiful ecru night gown. "Ooo la la," she says, holding it up to her shoulders. "You know how to spoil a girl."

"Maybe we're spoiling Johnny," Vee says with a wink.

The following day, she heads to work with a renewed sense of optimism. Miss Johnson is in a good mood, so Katie, Varydan and Vee tease about working in a "darn morgue!" Even Jane plays along.

The group meets Glenda at the Commerce for lunch.

"One last hoorah before you're married."

"Don't fret, Katie. You can't get rid of me that easy. I'll be back at the library after my honeymoon. Things will never change."

The only married woman at the table, Vee drops her eyes and mumbles, "Don't count on it. Marriage changes lots of things."

When Vee arrives home, Bob stands just inside the door with two packages in hand.

"What's this?"

Bob looks a bit disgruntled. "It's our anniversary."

Vee gasps. "Thank you! You're so sweet." She opens the larger box to find two silky white slips. The smaller box holds a beautiful pin.

All through dinner, Bob taunts her about forgetting.

"You better watch out," she cautions. "Don't make me sore at you. I warn you, there's a little Spanish in me."

Bob raises his eyebrows. "Is that so? Tell me who did it! I'll kill him!"

Even the twins laugh.

*February 1, 1946*
*Tampa, Florida*
*Dearest Vee,*

*How's every little thing out your way? We're having warm weather, thank goodness. The birds are singing and the trees have new green leaves; one would think it's the first signs of Spring*

*Vee, I was reading Gene's letters the day before yesterday, and they really made me blue. I'm not able to get him off my mind. Why did it have to happen to us. We loved each other so much. Every place I go, there's memories. Whenever they play Stardust I can't help but cry, we both liked it so much. It was our favorite song.*

*Please write soon, and send regards to Mom, Dad, and the children.*

*Love,*

*Carmen*

# HOME FRONT

# THIRTY-ONE

**The day after their anniversary, Bob hangs out during Vee's shift.** It is evident that he has no intention of finding work in the city, but keeps pressing for her to return to Harrisonville and to the farm. She cannot imagine anything more dull.

"But it's your duty as my wife," he says as they walk passed the store windows on the way home.

Vee ignores his comment and points at a woman's wool suit in Mindlin's window. "Look! That's almost like the one I bought last year."

"You won't need suits on the farm."

"But I love my job. Gosh, if it wasn't for the library, I'd go crazy."

Over the next two nights, Bob tries his best to make Vee happy. And even though he shares his best side, Vee keeps her emotions in check. One line of a song repeats in her head: "I keep wishing I were somewhere else."

On Saturday night, Vee decks out in her best evening clothes and goes alone to hear Sigmund Romberg in concert. Afterward, she gushes to Bob about the experience.

"It was the most beautiful thing I've ever heard! He played nearly every piece of sheet music I have including *Clair de Lune*. And oh, all four singers were super!"

Bob shrugs. "It all sounds the same to me."

Vee tries to sustain her enthusiasm. "Joseph Bell is grand. And one of the girls sang *Siboney*."

When Bob gives her a blank stare, Vee huffs and turns away. Not only do they have nothing in common, but the constant bickering is wearing thin. This is not a life she can tolerate much longer.

In the stacks at work, Vee sneaks glimpses of a book about the life of writer George Sand. She decides to check it out in earnest, splitting her time between it and another book that will influence her greatly—*Valley of Decision*. Caught up in them both, she realizes what she wants most from life. Autonomy. George Sand had achieved it a century earlier—changing her name from Amantine Lucile Aurore Dupin, wearing men's clothing, writing best-selling novels. The more she identifies with George, the more assertive she is with Bob. And the more tempers flare.

Valentine's Day, Vee grabs an orange, a cup of tea, and an iron pill for breakfast. She races to catch the street car and then settles into the ride with *The Life of George Sand*. When she takes off her coat at the library, she realizes her purse still sits on the streetcar bench.

"Oh, no!" she moans to Katie. "I do hope someone turns it in. What a miserable two days this has been."

"Why? What else has happened?"

Vee hangs her coat and pushes a strand of hair from her face. "You know that Bob and I haven't been getting on too well. We decided, simultaneously, to get down off the fence and go on the rocks."

"Oh, Vee. I'm sorry to hear that."

"I'm not. The fearful question is finally over—whether I will be his superior or his prisoner." She picks up a handful of returns and Katie follows her into the stacks.

"Are you sure this is what you want to do?"

Vee nods. "I won't live with a man I'm superior to, and my strong will won't let me be any man's prisoner. Besides, it's better now than in ten years when children would be involved."

Katie helps push a book onto one of the higher shelves. "Divorce. That's a really big step. It could make it harder to remarry."

"I do not expect to remarry." Vee thinks of Betty Corn and her resolve to stay single and become a doctor. "I never should have. Fate made us do so. And he was a kind and generous person, sweeter to me than anyone else had been." She keeps quiet about the change in Bob's personality.

"And Bob agreed?"

"Yes. It's the only way. I'd be crushed if I had to go back to the farm. I hope he sees it this way." Vee turns her back to the books and drops her shoulders. "I'm sorry for him. And for Loretta and his family and all the other people who won't be able to understand."

Katie gives Vee a warm hug. "As Kathleen says, sometimes we have battles we can't fight. We have to rise above them."

Back at the circulation desk, Miss Johnson leaves a box of Valentine's candy for the crew. At home, Bob gives Vee the nylons and gold earrings he had purchased a few days earlier, and then he says his goodbyes before heading to the bus station.

It is the right decision, Vee knows, but it still stirs melancholy in her heart. She quietly attends to her evening chores—washing clothes, her hair, ironing. With those duties out of the way, she sits down to write a handful of letters to the few friends who might understand her choices.

*March 4, 1946*
*Tampa, Florida*
*Dearest Vee,*

> *Say, what's up? Haven't heard from you in a while.*
>
> *Is your hubby home again? I guess he has his discharge by now. I do wish you could come down to Florida for your second honeymoon. You're more than welcome.*
>
> *A boy across the street came back from overseas last night. His aunt and the family want me to go out and show him the town. Never happen! Mother says he's good and kind like Gene, but I say he can't shine Gene's shoes. There'll never be one like him; never!!*
>
> *My brother has been in the hospital for nine days with a high fever and an infected throat. Thank God he's much better now.*
>
> *Did you get a look at Churchill and Truman? I heard their speeches. Don't breath it to a soul, but I'm all against what Truman said. He said you shouldn't eat as much as we've been doing, and if we have an abundance of something, we should divide it with the other nations. He should start at his home and then feed our own. There's many a family in the U.S. that go to bed at night with an empty stomach.*
>
> *Well, I'll close for now. Give Mom and Dad a hug and kiss for me and regards to the boys.*
>
> *Love and Lots of Luck,*
> *Carmen*

Work is what Vee lives for. Jane treats her like a little sister—mentoring her to the point that Vardyan accuses Jane of having a *pet*. Her coworkers keep up a stream of antics that give the often somber library the air of a comedy sketch.

"I called my housewife, Johnny, to see what he was doing," Glenda says. "Turns out, he was over at Mrs. Murdock's all morning exchanging recipes."

"You've got it lucky," Katie says. "A man who wants to do all the cooking."

"Maybe. The other day, he asked 'isn't our marriage certificate something like a driver's license? It expires in about two years?'"

Vee revels in a joy for living that she's missed for over two years. Her fellow librarians are not just a work family, but they meet her on an intellectual level new to her experience. And Loretta's family continues to host her without reservation or complaint.

She comes across a line attributed to George Sand: "It is not a material life, excitement, plays or fine clothes that I need, but liberty." It is true that Vee has developed a love of fine things, and she craves the culture that her city has to offer, but it is, indeed, liberty that she seeks.

Jeanie and Wayne Long pick her up one evening for a night on the town. When she returns home, Bob is waiting.

"I waited for you all evening. Where were you?"

The conversation takes on the tone of an inquisition. Vee can feel the vice of control suffocating her again. As the exchange escalates into another argument, Vee shuts him down with an angry retort. "Stop giving me a psychological test over every little detail of my life! As if I have to have a reason for every darn thing I say and do."

Bob entreats his wife to try again. She sends him back to Harrisonville with a firm *no* for an answer.

The news at work the next day strengthens her resolve. While Bob had been trying to reclaim his wife, Thelma's husband had beaten her so badly she can't walk.

To make matters worse, Jane finds out about the separation and scolds Vee. "I should paddle you both!" To get back into her good graces, Vee shops for the perfect birthday gift—a piece of jewelry to fit Jane's personality.

Time comes to formalize the separation. Vee rides the bus to Harrisonville and meets Bob in town. They talk over business matters but decide nothing. She agrees to ride out to her in-laws with the idea that she will return to the city that night, but her husband sabotages her plans. It is sheer agony spending time with his parents now that everyone knows. As her head throbs, she excuses herself and goes to bed.

In the morning, Bob finally agrees to take her to town. She stops in at a law office run by someone the family knows well. With the divorce papers filed, she returns to the city and tries to sleep away a migraine.

"At least I know which way I'm going again," she tells Loretta.

# HOME FRONT

# THIRTY-TWO

**V**ee builds a routine of work, time with friends, and helping Loretta with chores and the twins. Every spare moment, she listens to Nelson Eddy, James Milton, or Sigmund Romberg on the radio. She seldom thinks about her husband and the pressure he must be getting from family and friends to salvage his marriage. One evening, she opens her writing tablet and discovers a note that he had left hidden a few pages back. His persona on paper always tugs at her heart. Feeling a pang of guilt, she decides to write a return note.

Both Vee and Jane bring their worst tempers to work the following day. It is unusual for either one to be moody, but the fact that they are both lashing out disturbs Vee. They are not the only ones having a difficult day.

"I'm thinking of firing Mitch," Graves says when she arrives.

"Mitch?"

"My cleaning lady. She didn't show up this morning."

"How can you afford a cleaning lady on a library salary?"

"Oh, Mr. Graves pays for it. He's seen me keep house."

Around ten that morning, Mr. Graves calls to say that Mitch did not show up because she is in jail. She stabbed her husband to death the night before.

Jane shakes her head. "Just goes to show, life can always get worse."

Renewed correspondence with Bob brings a renewed push to reconcile their differences. The roller coaster takes its tole soon enough. There are few people in her life who support her, not to mention the stigma it will leave on her reputation.

The last day of March, Vee rides to Harrisonville. She taxis to her in-laws' and plays piano while she waits for the family to come home from church. When they arrive, they cannot have been more rude. Bob, their oldest son, can do no wrong, and now his wife has proven to be a selfish snob.

Vee bears the treatment bravely. Perhaps she deserves it. Bob, on the other hand, appears to enjoy stirring the pot. He treats his wife as if she has done no wrong which only serves to irritate his parents. After a lengthy discussion, Vee agrees to drop the divorce.

In the city, she stops at the library to give Miss Johnson her two-week's notice.

"Oh, my. We'll miss you, dear. You'll be a hard one to replace."

"I'm sorry to leave. I'll certainly miss everyone, especially Jane."

Discouraged, Miss Johnson puts her head in her hands. "We're all like one big happy family."

That night, Vee finishes *Valley of Decision*. It is hard for her to understand how any one woman can know so much about so many things. Perhaps a part of it is false—what is not part false? From her modest world view, she believes that the story delves into everything that could happen to any type of person, place, or country. And in some strange definite way it proves that one has to live as one feels. They have to have their individual emotional outlets—no matter how different they may be or how they may be accepted by others.

The next day, Katie takes Vee to lunch and they discuss happiness and what people live for. "It's certainly not library work as a profession."

"I don't know," Vee says, wistful. "As much as I love books, I could see myself here for the rest of my life. Give me a good book and a radio, and my heart is full."

Vee's last week is filled with anxiety. She continues to wonder if reconciliation is the right thing. She even begins to question George Sand's stance on life.

"Maybe it's great to be master of one's soul, but I'd like to be *cabin boy* for some object of my affection the rest of my natural life. Guess we can't have everything."

She will miss Jane the most, she has such love and respect for her. And then there is Loretta—the kindest, most generous person she has ever met. Not only did Loretta taken her in, but she has given her unconditional support at every turn.

"I like all the girls," Vardyan says on Thursday's break, "but I'm sorry you're leaving, cause I like you best."

On Friday, several of the girls treat Vee to lunch at the Westport Room in Union Station. Miss Grant gives her a pretty white sheer blouse. Katie and Vardyan, a beautiful gold compact so artistic it screams Vardyan's style.

"I won't ever forget this," she tells them. "Ever!"

Miss Grant pats Vee's hand. "I'm so afraid that my interest in the library is leaving with you, my dear."

Sunday morning, with just a few hours sleep, Vee catches the bus to Harrisonville. She stops at her grandmother's and then walks about town for a while. When Bob comes for her, they eat supper with Ella before attending Sunday evening service and then heading to the Beckerdite farm.

Monday morning, Bob drives Vee the mile to an old farmhouse that has sat empty for some time. Vee looks at the inside and cringes.

"It's a mess."

Bob starts a fire in the stove. "We can clean it up."

They spend some time sweeping in the room that will become the kitchen. Before Vee can remove the dirt, Bob grabs a small twig from the stove and sets the dust pile on fire.

"What are you doing?" Vee watches Bob walk off, but the pile simply smolders and dies. She scoops the remains from the wooden floor and carries them outside. "I guess that's the beauty of having something you can't hurt."

The couple buys paint, brooms, dishes, some cooking utensils. They pick up Vee's personal things stored in her old attic bedroom. Her dad works to straighten the crooked doors in the house. Trucil refinishes a beautiful mahogany dresser and mirror, and makes a coffee table and large dining table for his daughter's new home. Her mom sews curtains for the windows and seat covers for the chairs. The couple buys a new divan and picks out three linoleum pieces to cover the worn wooden floors.

Toward the end of the week, they make a quick trip to Kansas City to retrieve the last of Vee's things from Loretta and Ken's. It is hard to bid farewell to the city. Even harder to say goodbye to the family she has come to think of as her own.

Knowing how much she loves music, Bob buys Vee a radio, but in the evenings, they argue over the dial.

After a surprise belated wedding shower, Vee settles into a quiet routine—cooking, cleaning, listening to the radio. Waiting for her husband to come home. She fills her heart with as much connection as she can on Sundays, hoping it will sustain her through the week. Occasionally, she goes visiting with Bob or with her mother. Once a week, she walks the mile to her mother-in-law's to do the washing. Naomi has softened a bit toward her son's wife, so the time spent with the Beckerdites becomes bearable, even enjoyable again.

April turns to May. Vee naps frequently in the afternoons. Sometimes it is boredom. Sometimes, throbbing headaches debilitate her for hours. She hates it most when the headaches interfered with her ability to socialize.

*May 13, 1946*
*Tampa, Florida*
*My Dearest Vee,*

> *It has been a long long time since I have heard from you. I couldn't write sooner cause I've been rather busy lately. I work during the day, and then I go to night school. I like my job very much. I work with a urology doctor, and it's very interesting.*

> *How are Mom and Dad and the boys? Did Mom every receive the Flying Cross that belonged to Gene? How I miss him. I miss him more as days roll by.*

> *How's your hubby? You hurry up and come down. Of course, you'd get sunburnt quick with this Florida sunshine, but you would enjoy the beach.*

> *Well, Vee, write and tell me the latest dope about movies, operas or anything of interest. Give the folks my regards.*

> *As Ever,*
> *Carmen*


Vee opens the bottom drawer of the beautiful mahogany dresser her parent's had given them. From beneath her clothes, she removes a large bundle tied up in ribbon. It contains packets of letters from Gene, Wayne, and Carmen. Sliding the latest into place, she looks down at three diaries—1944, 1945, and the one in which she will make her latest entry. Flipping through the pages, she recalls the heartaches, the forever friendships, the many difficult decisions she has had to make since boarding a train to marry a man who deserves better than a woman who will simply settle for farm life.

The previous pages overflow with her observations and desires. She had filled each page until her scribbles spilled onto the margins and she had had to find more bare pages to exhaust her thoughts. But today, she simply writes, "Bob promised to get me a little dog to keep me company."

Closing the diary, she places it with the others beneath her clothing and shuts the drawer.

# POSTSCRIPT

**D**espite a tumultuous relationship, Velma and Robert built a successful construction business made possible, in large part, from a sum Velma inherited from her grandfather. The couple raised four wonderful children—Annette, Charles *Eugene*, Melinda, and James. They divorced twenty-nine years later.

Now alone in her fifties, Velma made a good life for herself. She returned to the workforce as an inspector in a plastics factory—work reminiscent of her War years. She traveled the United States extensively with family and friends, and took overseas trips to China, The Netherlands, and Russia.

When Velma turned 70, she and Wayne Long—whose wife had passed away four years earlier—ran into each other one morning and decided to have breakfast together. As they talked over old times, breakfasts became dinners. Dinners became weekend trips. And for the last seventeen years of Velma's life, Wayne was the kind and generous companion she had missed out on for so long. Even then, she maintained her independence to the end.

Velma and Betty Corn wrote to each other for the rest of their lives—sharing regular letters and even visiting a few times.

Five years after Gene was killed in action, his remains were recovered by the U.S. military and reburied in France. A year earlier, his fiancé Carmen sent Velma a wedding invitation. She had found the courage to move on. Though the two women never met in person, they, too, stayed in touch through Christmas cards and letters until Carmen passed away.

On vacation in her early eighties, Velma and daughter Anne stopped at the Pioneer Museum in Nebraska. There, she saw a Pratt & Whitney engine like the ones she helped build during WWII. It was a moment of pride and reflection. Only after she died at the age of eighty-seven did her family find the Nineteen-Forties diaries and the letters from Eugene, Carmen, and Wayne—significant for the role Velma played on the home front and precious because of the connection to her lost brother. This book is to honor her sacrifices.

Vee at six months old—the baby picture she wanted to send to the "best [publishing] houses."

Trucil and Minnie with baby Eugene (Gene).

Trucil and Minnie with baby Harold Dean (HD).

Gene, HD, and Vee around the time their mother Minnie died of appendicitis.
Gene, HD, and Vee outside the house they lived in before The Great Depression.
The blended family—Trucil and Mildred's children. Front row: HD, Bill and Bob (Hedrick);
back row: Vee and Gene. All of the step children remained close throughout their lives.

The log home Trucil built on the smaller acreage he managed to keep by giving the rest of his property to the bank during The Depression. When Trucil built a second, larger, concrete block home a short distance away in 1947, the cabin was used as a barn.

Mildred and Trucil. They married a few years after Vee's mother passed away. Mildred became "Mom" to her step-children, loving them as her own.

Gene's high school graduation photo.

Vee's high school graduation photo.

Vee in a pinafore she made, wearing a set of wings from her fiance Bob who was enlisted in the Army Air Corps.

Gene at the San Marcos Army Air Field in 1943. He had lost a flight log out of an open window and wasn't too happy when this photo was taken.

Echelon Two at the San Marcos Army Air Field in 1943.
Gene is the second from the left in the second row.

Gene at Harlingen Army Gunnery School in May of 1943.

Vee and Bob's wedding photo, January 1944.

Gene at Mac Dill Field, Tampa, Florida, where he met Carmen del Llano, 1944. He was missing his "big deal hat" that had been run over by a carnival ride on a date with Carmen.

Carmen del Llano, Gene's fiance.

Sophia Barbara, Vee's cousin whose family moved
to Hollywood for her singing and acting career.

Sophia Barbara. She had an 8x10 glossy portfolio taken hoping for work in the movies. She did land some singing and acting jobs on the radio.

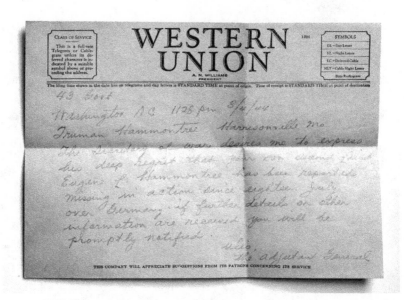

The August 4th telegram from the War Department stating that
Gene had gone missing a second time in 1944.

The second Purple Heart certificate for Eugene Lee Hammontree.

IN GRATEFUL MEMORY OF

Second Lieutenant Eugene C. Hammontree

WHO DIED IN THE SERVICE OF HIS COUNTRY

in the European Area, July 18, 1944

HE STANDS IN THE UNBROKEN LINE OF PATRIOTS WHO HAVE DARED TO DIE

THAT FREEDOM MIGHT LIVE, AND GROW, AND INCREASE ITS BLESSINGS.

FREEDOM LIVES, AND THROUGH IT, HE LIVES—

IN A WAY THAT HUMBLES THE UNDERTAKINGS OF MOST MEN

*Harry Truman*

PRESIDENT OF THE UNITED STATES OF AMERICA

The letter from President Harry Truman offering condolences for the family's sacrifice.

Mrs. Robert Beckerdite
1 9 4 6

A prayer - By Anon

Am I worth dying for?
Have I the right to claim
Some soldier's life, or
will he have died in vain?

Oh, God! Give me the wisdom,
courage to open the door
where I may find the things
that make me worth dying
for.

C H

Battle doesn't determine
who is right. Only who
is left.

Inside cover of Velma's 1946 diary. The "Prayer" she indicated that was by an anonymous poet has similarities to a poem Eleanor Roosevelt carried in her wallet until she died.

Vee's diary entries spilling to the top of the pages. She rarely left a space empty until moving back to the farm in 1946.

An example of many of Vee's diary entries once she left Kansas City and moved to the farm with husband Bob.

Velma at eighty standing beside the same type of Pratt & Whitney
airplane engine she made gears for during World War II.

A few of Gene's pins and medals.

# HOME FRONT